ADVANCED
MOTORCYCLING

ADVANCED MOTORCYCLING

The art of better motorcycle riding and
advanced motorcycling techniques compiled
by the Institute of Advanced Motorists

Second Edition

Published in association with the
Institute of Advanced Motorists.

*The male pronoun has been used throughout this book. This stems from a desire
to avoid ugly and cumbersome language, and no discrimination, prejudice or bias
is intended.*

**Cover photograph reproduced by kind permission of BMW (GB) Ltd. Pictured is a
BMW K100RS, with riders clothed in BMW Sprint leather suits and BMW System II
helmets.**

First published in 1977 by Queen Anne Press,
3rd Floor, Greater London House, Hampstead Road,
London NW1 7QX.

Reprinted 1978
Reprinted 1979
Revised and updated 1982
Reprinted 1983
Reprinted 1986

This revised and updated edition first published in 1989 by
Kogan Page Ltd, 120 Pentonville Road, London N1 9JN
in association with the Institute of Advanced Motorists,
IAM House, 359/365 Chiswick High Road, London W4 4HS.
Text Consultant: Rod Collins
Printed and bound in Great Britain by
Richard Clay, The Chaucer Press, Bungay

British Library Cataloguing in Publication Data
Advanced motorcycling.– 2nd ed.
1. Motorcycles. Riding. Manuals
I. Institute of Advanced Motorists
629.28'475

ISBN 1–85091–914–3

Contents

Foreword   viii
Preface   x

1. Introduction – The Need for Advanced Riding   1

Pursuit testing 2; The Institute of Advanced Motorists (IAM) 2; Aiming for Improvement 3

2. Thinking Ahead   4

The benefits of planning 4; Concentration and pre-planning 4; Commentary riding 6; Your state of mind 7; Tolerance and courtesy 7; Summary 7

3. The Systematic Method   9

A procedure for all hazards 9; Summary 13

4. Observation   14

Your eyesight 14; Observation ahead 15; Observation behind 18; Mirrors 19; Road surface 20; Selective observation 21; Summary 24

5. Positioning   25

Exceptions to the 'keep left' rule 25; Positioning on bends 28; Summary 31

6. Cornering   32

Cornering forces 32; Control through bends 34; Positioning on bends 35; Summary 37

7. Braking in Wet and Dry Conditions   39

Use of front and rear brakes 39; Braking distance 41; Braking on a bend 42; Discs and Drums 43; Summary 45

8. Gearchanging   46

Use of the gearbox 46; Slowing down 48; Acceleration 49; Summary 50

9. Overtaking   51

When to overtake 51; Overtaking technique 54; Summary 56

10. Junctions   57
Crossroads 57; Traffic lights 60; Roundabouts 61;
Summary 64

11. Signals   65
Direction indicators 66; Hand signals 67; The
headlight 68; The brake light 69; Horn 70; Summary
71

12. Road-craft in Town and Country   72
Riding in town 72; Riding in the country 76; Summary
80

13. Motorways   81
Terminology 82; Joining a motorway 82; Motorway
discipline 83; Lane discipline 83; Keep your distance
84; Overtaking 84; Changing lanes 85; Slip road
courtesy 85; Abnormal motorway conditions 85;
Leaving the motorway 89; Keeping your motorcycle
in trim 90; Summary 91

14. Economical Riding   93
The motorcycle you buy 93; Techniques for economy
94; Summary 96

15. Night Riding   97
Lighting equipment 97; Eyesight and fatigue 98;
Dazzle and visibility 99; Summary 103

16. Seasonal Variations   104
Riding in winter 104; Riding in summer 109;
Summary 111

17. Fog   113
Speed and vision 113; Being seen 114; Traffic 114;
Summary 116

18. Reaction Times   118
Your reactions 118; Other people's reactions 121;
Summary 122

19. Accidents   123
Stop and think 123; Park safely 123; Warn other road
users 124; Send for help 124; Answer these questions
124; Dial 999 125; Give this information 125; Help the
casualties 127; Get first aid training 128; Carry a first
aid kit 128; Fire 128; Accident procedures 129;
Protecting yourself 131; Summary 132

20. Pillion Passengers and Sidecars   **133**

Pillion passengers 133; Sidecars 135; Summary 137

21. Understanding the Machine   **138**

Understanding your motorcycle 138; Sympathy with your motorcycle 142; Summary 143

22. Tyres   **144**

Looking after your tyres 144; Tyre technicalities 149; Summary 151

23. Clothing   **152**

The need for good clothing 152; Choosing your clothing 153; Summary 158

24. Helmets   **159**

Helmet styles 159; Straps, visors and goggles 161; Summary 162

25. Touring Abroad   **163**

Planning ahead 163; Differences to watch for 165; Summary 168

26. Now for the Test   **169**

The advanced motorcycling test 169; What does the test involve? 171; Who can take the test? 171; Where can I take the test? 172; Who are the examiners? 172; Results 175; When you pass 175

List of Test Routes   **176**

Signs and Signals   **179**

Signs giving orders 181; Warning signs 182; Direction signs 183; Information signs 185; Light signals controlling traffic 186; Road markings 187

FOREWORD

The pleasure that a motorcycle can give to its rider by its efficiency and economy of effort is offset by every motorcyclist's awareness that any accident may well prove extremely painful and possibly permanently disabling. A motorcycle rider therefore has to anticipate potential dangers and deal with unfavourable conditions with a much greater degree of accuracy than a car driver, surrounded as the latter is by a protective barrier of bodywork. A motorist risks dents in his bodywork in an accident – a motorcyclist risks life and limb.

The skill which any motorcyclist needs to survive on our increasingly crowded and treacherous roads is more instinctive than theoretical, yet the author of this fully revised and updated manual has managed to describe the necessary skill in brief, well-chosen phrases, and to relate his good advice concerning the road conditions so familiar to us all, describing the hazards to be avoided in clear, simple terms.

I can see that this book will help to make our roads safer for all those people who choose to travel on two wheels rather than on four, and I hope that, together with the Institute of Advanced Motorists' advanced motorcycling test, it will help to reduce those sinister statistics which relate to motorcycle accidents.

Passing a test does not necessarily prove that the rider will always maintain the standards of riding that the test has called for, but the intellectual effort needed to achieve such a standard should become second nature to that rider, and this will help him to function more effectively in hazardous situations.

Insurance companies have been known to acknowledge the statistical reliability of those who have passed the advanced test. I therefore hope to take the advanced motorcycle test shortly, and I know I will find this manual invaluable as a very readable alternative to a 'crash course' in advanced motorcycling!

H.R.H. The Duke of Gloucester, GCVO
President, Institute of Advanced Motorists

PREFACE

Looking back on the days before I decided to do my racing on circuits instead of roads, I shudder to think of what might have happened. Today, I still see riders (and four-wheel motorists, for that matter) who treat the open highway as their own personal race circuit.

We motorcyclists are the most susceptible of road users – for obvious reasons. As a result, we need to take heed of all the advice we can get, which is why I endorse the practical recommendations made in this fully revised edition of *Advanced Motorcycling*. It is much too easy for someone to get his licence without fully appreciating the skills that safe motorcycling demands. Skills come from training and experience, and one way of developing these qualities is through the Institute of Advanced Motorists' motorcycle test, which I have taken myself. For those just starting out on motorcycles, I recommend strongly the RAC/ACU training scheme.

I must stress, however, that there is no substitute for common sense when it comes to riding bikes. For example, it is plain good sense to keep a safe distance when you're following another vehicle. Not only do you give yourself the necessary time to stop; you are able to look ahead properly to danger spots, such as patches of water or loose gravel, that could so easily upset you.

While books and training courses can teach the principles, at the same time they cannot teach natural ability and instinct. The majority of riders possess these, but they need to develop them. Get to know your machine; become part of it; establish a relationship with it. Everything on your bike is there for your use, and the more you become attuned to your bike, the easier and safer it is to ride.

One last point. When you're riding, help other motorists to see you. Drive with dipped headlight during the day, and wear fluorescent protective clothing. Don't skimp on clothing and helmets. Buy the best you can afford because they will give you the best protection.

Safety makes sense, and it will increase the enjoyment that I hope everyone who reads this book will derive from motorcycling.

Phil Read

1

INTRODUCTION – THE NEED FOR ADVANCED RIDING

The last decade has seen a marked decline in the number of new motorcycles sold annually in Britain, from over 250,000 at the start of the 1980s to around 90,000 today. This does not entirely reflect a decline in motorcycle usage, however, for it suggests that riders are holding on to their machines and not changing them so frequently, and more recently there have been encouraging signs of a revival. It might also indicate that the glamorous 150mph superbikes, marketed by all the Japanese manufacturers and some of the Europeans, appeal to a smaller and smaller minority. It could be postulated that riders are tired of year-by-year model changes.

Whatever the state of the market, there is a greater need than ever before for advanced motorcycling techniques. The gains in car performance – as well as the advent of safety features like anti-lock brakes, low-profile tyres, crumple zones and strengthened passenger 'cages' – induce drivers to travel faster, to leave less braking distance and to corner nearer the limit. All this makes it more difficult for the average rider to stay out of trouble, and emphasises the need for defensive motorcycle road-craft. To be fair to our fellow road users, similar advances in superbike design – especially in steering, suspension and tyre adhesion – encourage the imprudent rider to explore the limits of cornering, leaving no margin for error.

Even though there is increasing emphasis on primary training and more restrictions planned for learner and inexperienced riders, nearly 1000 riders, passengers and pedestrians lose their lives every year in motorcycle accidents. There is a 1 in 60 chance that an accident on two wheels will prove fatal. Compared with the odds against death or serious injury in a car accident, this makes motorcycling look a very dangerous pastime. Yet it need not be so. Many riders, perhaps after one or two 'scrapes' early in their riding careers, manage to get through a whole lifetime of riding without coming to harm. The techniques they use to stay alive are outlined in this book.

Pursuit testing

Traditionally, the would-be motorcyclist has been left very much to his own devices, but the Department of Transport's ever-increasing interest in promoting rider training is bringing important changes. Primary rider training, the British Motorcycle Federation's forte for many years, seems certain to become compulsory for new riders, and pursuit testing is likely to be adopted by the Department of Transport (DoT) soon after this book is published. At least the learner will be able to demonstrate his skills to a rider instead of a pedestrian examiner. This last proposal endorses the philosophy of the IAM's advanced test, which has always been a one-to-one situation with the candidate being followed by the examiner on his own machine.

The Institute of Advanced Motorists (IAM)

The IAM was founded in 1956 by motorists from all walks of life, with the common aim of making our roads safer by raising driving standards. It has succeeded to an impressive extent. Over 300,000 motorists have taken the advanced driving test, and some 70 per cent of them have passed and become members of the IAM. A survey by the Government's Transport and Road Research Laboratory (TRRL) has shown that those who are successful have, on average, a 25 per cent lower accident rate than those who fail, and a 50 to 70 per cent better record than the general motoring public. IAM members, adds the TRRL survey, not only have fewer accidents, but those in which they are involved tend to be less serious. Nowadays the IAM's activities have expanded to include motorcyclists, setting high standards of skill at which responsible riders can aim by taking the advanced test at any venue in the national network of test centres.

Aiming for improvement

No motorcyclist is perfect in the way he handles his machine, no more than any car driver is perfect. Passing the Government test is merely the completion of your apprenticeship, and the beginning of a new learning process in which basic skills are refined and developed in order that you can become a master craftsman. This book is aimed at those motorcyclists, like yourself, who are sensible enough to acknowledge that aspects of their riding can be improved. It aims to provide all the information necessary for you to make sure that your best workmanship always goes into the art of riding safely. Whether you use your motorcycle for essential journeys or just for pleasure, remember that riding safely and skilfully is far more satisfying than riding dangerously; it also gives you a much better chance of enjoying a full lifetime of riding.

Much of what follows concentrates on riding technique, but advice about safety-related aspects such as maintenance, clothing and tyres is also included. Do remember that *Advanced Motorcycling* is a practical guide to riding, not a legal textbook. It does not aim to provide a detailed survey of rules and regulations. The *Highway Code* is the basis for learning; *Advanced Motorcycling* completes your riding course.

Many younger riders believe that motorcycling is either fun or safe: advanced riding will show you how to combine safety with skill, and open the door to enjoyable motorcycling.

THINKING AHEAD

All road users need to adopt a planned and systematic approach to the handling of their vehicles, but this is doubly important for a motorcyclist. A prerequisite of good riding is the ability to concentrate on the conditions around you and anticipate what lies ahead so that every manoeuvre is carried out in good time and under complete control. Experience improves a rider's skill in planning his actions, but the need to concentrate and anticipate must never be underestimated. Every time you alter course, accelerate, change gear or brake, your safety depends upon positive planning.

The benefits of planning

Unlike a car, a motorcycle is inherently unstable on its two wheels: leave it alone and it will fall over, upset the delicate balance of forces while it is moving and it will fall over and take you with it. The best way to remain upright and in complete control of a motorcycle is to avoid sudden changes in the relationship between road surface and tyre – fierce braking, hard acceleration, bad gearchanging, sudden changes of course, etc. This means thinking ahead so that each change of condition is affected smoothly and gradually.

Concentration and pre-planning

Steady concentration and thinking ahead gives an added bonus in reducing wear and tear on your machine. If you ride smoothly and thoughtfully, many of the mechanical parts of your motorcycle – tyres, brake pads, gears, chain, clutch, even the engine itself – will last longer and need less frequent maintenance. It may be stretching a point to suggest that a bike reacts like a horse to sensitive riding, but experienced motorcyclists would surely agree that smooth and intelligent use of a bike gives great satisfaction from the rapport between rider and machine, as well as improving safety.

Your motorcycle can become almost an extension of your body, as ready to react to your commands as an arm or a finger. If you consistently plan ahead, your machine can always be in the right gear on the right part of the road and travelling at the right speed. Other factors – such as careful observation, good control techniques and road sense – are also necessary, but developing the ability to anticipate potential hazards is essential to safe motorcycling. No matter how well a rider can control his machine in a dangerous situation, he is safer if he can foresee a hazard and prepare himself accordingly.

Besides giving you complete mastery over your machine regardless of conditions, concentration and thinking ahead also enable you to spot little details of other people's activity. Let us use an example to illustrate the point. Without complete concentration you could be taken by surprise if a child runs into your path, forcing you to react suddenly with a grasp of the front brake lever and a stab on the rear brake pedal. You miss the child and ride on, a little shaken and cursing the youngster's lack of care. But you should be honest with yourself: surely the child's appearance could have been anticipated? Maybe that sign which you failed to take in a few hundred yards back warned of a school? That group of people standing by a gate must have been mothers waiting for their children. And it is 3.30 in the afternoon – going-home time. With 100 per cent concentration you would have been prepared for the unexpected.

It is a good exercise to look back on any journey, long or short, to review the number of sudden actions which you had to take. Think through the circumstances of each one and ask yourself how many potential accidents could have been avoided with a more concentrated, planned response to road and traffic conditions. Good riders avoid rather than survive accidents by predicting all possible occasions when they might be caused by other road-users.

Commentary riding

The Institute of Advanced Motorists has always recommended that car drivers should practise 'commentary driving', although this is no longer an obligatory part of the advanced test. As an advanced motorcyclist you can also benefit from this technique, for it gives you a very clear understanding of your anticipation of events and your response to them. Do not worry about what other people might think if they see you talking to yourself under your helmet! A typical commentary might sound like this:

Green light, move away and accelerate steadily through the gears – watch speed as this is a built up area – parked lorry ahead, so check mirror and signal change of course – pull out in good time, covering horn button as someone could be hidden behind lorry, needing warning of my approach – pedestrian crossing ahead, people around so someone might wish to cross – check mirror in case signals and braking are necessary – change down a gear for slight incline – potholes in the road and loose gravel coming up – brake gently in advance and keep a straight course, more weight on footrests to absorb shock – over those, relax but keep concentrating – expect to be turning right after next bend, so check mirror – red Ford suddenly close behind, might overtake – let him go, but careful around bend in case he brakes hard to take same right turn – mirror again, signal right turn before bend – change down, select course near continuous centre line – lift bike up after bend before braking and changing down again – keep speed down, in second gear, ready to make turn through that safe gap after stream of oncoming traffic.

At first you will almost certainly be amazed how much of this sort of detailed planning and concentration you have neglected in the past. With a little practice, however, you should surprise yourself with how much more observant you become. Assessing all the informtion and potential hazards around you long before you reach them is one of the fundamentals of advanced motorcycling.

Your state of mind

Commentating is an especially good discipline if you find a particular journey dull or if you are tired at the end of a day's work – at times like these concentration may lapse, allowing dangerous situations to develop before you become aware of them. It is vital that you should always ride in a clear state of mind, and the realisation of this is one of the secrets of advanced motorcycling. While the exhilaration and enjoyment of riding are rightly savoured by motorcyclists, these emotions should never be indulged at the expense of a calm and tolerant attitude. The aggression which some irresponsible riders show to other road users has no place in advanced motorcycling: riding with self-control is not only the most satisfying way, but also the safest. By the same token, it should be mentioned that a timid approach can be just as dangerous as an aggressive one, for accidents can be caused by indecision and failure to take prompt action when faced with a situation demanding quick thinking.

Tolerance and courtesy

You should take pride in being a tolerant and courteous rider at all times. Even the most mild-mannered people become irritated, or even angry, when other road users – particularly those car drivers with seemingly no regard for the safety of motorcyclists – behave stupidly or inconsiderately. Never let your own riding standard be affected, and remember that your behaviour may act as an example. Whatever the aggravation, it is much safer to resist any temptaion to retaliate. Stay calm, stay in control, and stay alive.

Summary

- Complete *concentration* and *planning ahead* are essential ground rules for safe motorcycling; the ability to predict the possible actions of other road users will usually keep you out of trouble.

- Practise *commentary riding* so that you regularly monitor your powers of observation and anticipation.
- Always be aware of the importance of your *state of mind* when riding: have a calm and tolerant attitude at all times.

3

THE SYSTEMATIC METHOD

A systematic approach to every manoeuvre you make on your motorcycle goes hand in hand with the need to think ahead. Close examination of the causes of accidents involving motorcycles shows that in most cases the rider makes an error at some point in the sequence, allowing events over which he has no control to overtake him. Although he may react wrongly when an instant decision is called for, very often the mistake which leads to an accident – perhaps the failure to glance in the mirror or reduce speed soon enough – occurs very early in the sequence. The demands made on a rider's concentration by heavy traffic conditions make it all too easy to forget part of the basic procedure, and even experienced riders can make the initial errors which lead to accidents. However, just because you have been able to get away with these occasional mistakes so far does not mean that you will be equally lucky throughout your motorcycling career.

A procedure for all hazards

An advanced rider minimises the chance of making errors as far as is humanly possible by applying a systematic procedure whenever he needs to change speed or course. Whether a hazard is a bend, a junction or just a parked vehicle, the following sequence of actions should be considered:

1. *Course*
   Glance behind or check in your mirrors whenever you plan to change direction. Give a signal if

necessary before taking up the correct position on the road.

2. *Rear observation, signals and brakes*
   Check the conditions behind you, give any signals necessary to inform other road users of your intentions, and then brake to ensure that you approach the hazard at a safe speed.

3. *Gear*
   Select the appropriate gear to match your speed during the approach to the hazard.

4. *Rear observation and signal*
   Again, check behind and make any signals necessary to inform following traffic of your intentions.

5. *Horn*
   Use your horn if necessary to warn other people of your approach: people you can see may be unaware of your presence, and there may be people out of your sight who need to know that you are coming.

6. *Rear observation*
   Your final look behind is often termed the 'life saver': it is a last check that following drivers have noticed your intentions and are reacting accordingly.

7. *Acceleration*
   Once your motorcycle is on a straight course after negotiating the hazard, accelerate again to a cruising speed appropriate to road and traffic conditions.

Spelled out in detail this may seem like a complicated procedure, but in practice this systematic method is simple, quick and necessary. Putting it into action time and time again will soon make it almost instinctive. The system is not rigid: some circumstances may call for extra checks in the mirrors before braking, while others may require only some parts of the drill. By imposing this discipline on yourself and thinking well ahead, you will never be caught out by unexpected developments on the road ahead or involved in difficulties caused by another road user.

In addition to this, your planned method greatly reduces the danger of other road users being surprised by your actions. The familiar excuse from guilty car drivers, 'I didn't know he was going to turn right and it seemed safe to pass', can never be valid if you make sure that your

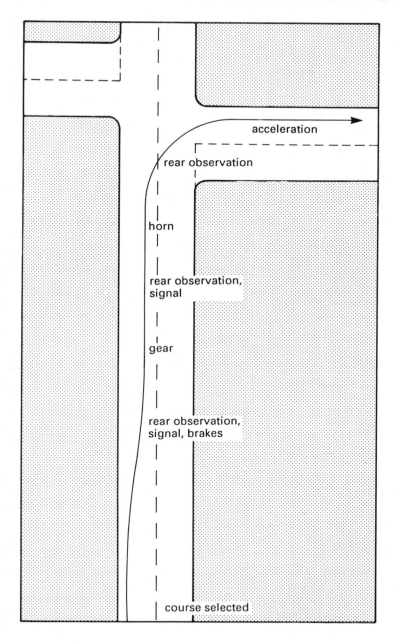

The correct sequence of events in planned, systematic riding at a junction

intentions are always clear. As well as keeping other road users informed, it is just as important to keep checking that they have seen you and are reacting correctly.

Throughout this book we shall refer back to this basic system, but it may help at this stage to illustrate how it is applied to a standard manoeuvre. Since right turns cause so many motorcycle accidents, this is the one we shall select. The diagram shows the approach to a simple junction and the stages at which the seven points of the system are considered, as follows:

1. *Course*
   Check behind and signal before moving towards the correct course: near the white centre line on a normal width road, further to the left on a narrower road. This course towards the crown of the road should be taken smoothly and evenly, not with a sudden swerve.

2. *Rear observation, signals, brakes*
   Once on your correct course, check behind again, show your intention with the indicators or a hand signal, and apply the brakes if necessary to reduce speed. If the road is wide enough, following traffic will be able to pass on the inside.

3. *Gear*
   The correct gear is selected after braking.

4. *Rear observation and signal*
   Another check to the rear and continue your signal if necessary.

5. *Horn*
   Sound the horn if it seems necessary before you have a clear view through the turn.

6. *Rear observation*
   Take a last look behind (the 'life saver') to check for an overtaking vehicle to your right before making the turn at a steady speed. Remember that pedestrians may be crossing at junctions.

7. *Acceleration*
   Build up speed again once your bike is straight to a level appropriate to road and traffic conditions.

Although this all seems rather long-winded when written down step by step, remember that it is simple to put into practice. Once mastered, it forms the basis for all advanced riding techniques.

Summary

- Absorb the *systematic method* outlined in this chapter: it is used whenever you need to change speed or course, and forms the basis for advanced riding.
- Remember that there are two major reasons for using this method: you are always prepared for *unexpected developments*, and other road users are never *surprised by your actions*.

4

OBSERVATION

Good powers of observation, which demand practice and thought, can keep you out of trouble in 90 per cent of all potentially dangerous incidents. You need to absorb all the information you see around and ahead of you when you ride, and select what is useful. All riders do this to a certain extent, but the advanced rider sees far more than the main features of his surroundings, for example road contours, junctions, traffic lights and so on. He has developed his road sense into an art, so that he is constantly assessing the changing road and traffic conditions around him. Just as a ship's master reads his chart in difficult waters, the advanced rider must read the road ahead to plot a safe course and speed, and anticipate potential hazards.

Your eyesight

Making sure that your vision is satisfactory is the first step you must take. Research has shown that an alarming number of riders have eyesight deficiencies, yet many of them are totally unaware that anything is wrong. Eyesight usually deteriorates so gradually that someone can have a potentially dangerous defect in his vision and perhaps compensate for it subconsciously. People who try to avoid riding at night because they are not happy about their vision in darkness ought to acknowledge that their daylight vision might also be less than perfect.

There are many eyesight problems which can affect a rider's safety. Having little or no sharp sight in one eye prevents good judgement of distance. Tunnel vision, the tendency to concentrate only on the view directly ahead and remain oblivious to anything more than a few degrees to the side, does not affect the ability to distinguish objects straight ahead in the distance, yet it seriously restricts the powers of observation which every rider must have. Good peripheral sight is essential in order to see out of the corner of the eye what is happening on either side of the bike. Long sight and short sight are extremely common (and proportionately worse at night), yet too many riders remain unaware of it until eventually they are forced to have an eye test. Colour blindness also causes serious problems, particularly if it takes the form of an inability to distinguish red; as well as brake lights and traffic lights, red is used for all danger signs on the road.

If you have not been to an optician for two years it would be wise to go for a proper check, whether or not you already wear spectacles. There will probably be nothing wrong – if there is, however, it would be better to find out now rather than after a serious accident caused by your defective sight. Eyesight deterioration can usually be corrected with contact lenses or glasses, the latter often with lenses and frames suitable for motorcycing. Make sure that the frame you select fits comfortably inside your full-face helmet, or use one-piece ski-type goggles if you wear an open-face helmet. If you already need glasses, you must remember that it is an offence to ride a motorcycle without wearing them.

After an unnecessary period of confusion and frustration over new regulations concerning eye protection, most riders accept that stricter control of visor and goggles standards has been a sensible move. Your visor or goggles should be to BS4110, to be legal and to give reasonable resistance to scratching. If you prefer a graded-tint visor, remember that it can be used legally only in daylight. No sensible rider will lament the disappearance of the very dark visor, although there is still the anomaly of sunglasses being legal. You can combat problems of misting, especially if you wear glasses, by treating the surfaces of the visor with a trace of washing-up liquid or a proprietary anti-mist compound.

Observation ahead

There tends to be some confusion over the correct use of rear observation: some old hands say that you should

The top far left *photo shows the view from behind the steering head of a person with average eyesight. Everything is clear, and peripheral vision is adequate.* Top, left *shows the effect of long-sightedness, with the foreground blurred and the distant objects in focus. Short-sightedness is even worse, as is illustrated by the picture,* bottom far left. *Everything ahead of you is dangerously blurred. Tunnel vision,* bottom, left *is a less common defect, but potentially disastrous. The view straight ahead is fine, but peripheral vision is badly affected. Finally, some people suffer from double vision,* right, *which can greatly affect your judgement on the road. If you suffer from these or other defects, it is in your own interest, as well as that of all other road users, to do something about it.*

never look over your shoulder on the motorway, while at the other end of the spectrum primary instructors encourage their pupils to look behind at virtually every lamp-post. The essence of rear observation is based on flexibility. What am I looking for? What can be expected? Is it safe to take my eyes off the road ahead? All these questions need to be answered. Some definitions might be helpful:

- *Life-saver*: the classic road-craft/police rider over-the-shoulder glance before turning right or left.
- *Shoulder check*: a less pronounced rearward glance to check the offside or nearside blind spots.

- *Mirror check*: use of the mirrors to perform rearward observation – note that sometimes this will require a change of position to obtain a total rearward view.
- *Rear observation*: the process of finding out what is behind you in the 180 degree arc from the handlebar ends rearwards.

Some inexperienced riders look at the part of the road immediately in front of them, thereby failing to notice sufficiently early the approach of junctions, roundabouts, changes in the road surface, parked cars and any other potential hazards. You should concentrate your gaze on a point some way ahead, while at the same time taking in events even further in the distance in addition to those closer to you and on either side.

This selective vision requires concentration and has to be developed with practice, so it is a good idea to train yourself to cast an eye over as wide a field of vision as possible. By this means your peripheral vision can take in a dog on the verge at the same time as you watch the move of an overtaking car in the distance. Your centre of focus must be adjusted constantly according to speed and how far ahead the road is visible.

Observation behind

You must also be observant about what is going on behind you, especially as drivers so often fail to see a motorcyclist. All motorcycles sold in Britain are now equipped with a pair of mirrors, so these remove some of the need to turn round to see behind. While it used to be the case that mirrors were often rendered useless by vibration, advances in motorcycle design – led by BMW and the Japanese manufacturers – have made today's machines far smoother than their predecessors, making mirrors a very useful part of any bike's equipment. If you buy a second-hand bike, it is possible that the mirrors might have disappeared through theft or breakage, so replace them as a matter of urgency.

Mirrors

Problems with vibration may have largely disappeared, but the dictates of styling and semi-race fairings have resulted in many modern bikes having poorly positioned mirrors which do not give a clear rearward view. Sometimes it is possible to move the mirrors outwards by packing out their mounting plates, or by cutting the stalks and extending them with short lengths of tubing suitably threaded or welded in place. There are signs of sanity returning on the most recent models, but there is still a long way to go. Of course, there are exceptions: the mirrors on Kawasaki GTRs, BMW K100RT and Honda Gold Wing are as near to being perfectly positioned as any rider could wish. Bar-end mounted mirrors can be used on some machines, but many multi-cylinder types now have anti-vibration weights in their bar ends which should not be discarded.

From both the safety and pleasure points of view, it is important to be able to glance easily at the road behind without having to crook your head or twitch your shoulder out of the way. Inevitably there will be blind spots in your rearward vision, so adjust your mirrors to minimise these. Get to know the blind spots for your machine by checking them out on a quiet road.

However good your mirrors, there are many occasions when an old-fashioned turn of the head is essential. As well as being a thoroughly good idea whenever you need to reassure yourself that a vehicle is not lurking in a blind spot, a quick glance over your shoulder is often a worthwhile precaution, particularly when about to overtake or pull away from rest. But do make it a *quick* glance, since you can cover a great deal of ground while you are looking behind: at 60mph, for example, your bike travels 88 feet in a second. Looking behind, either by turning round or using the mirrors, always carries with it a slight risk because your attention is not on the road ahead, so observe really carefully what is going on in order that one look does not have to be followed unnecessarily quickly by another. Needless to say, you should not be sitting so close to the vehicle in front that you have to worry about the possible consequences of momentarily looking behind.

Road surface

The condition of the road surface is a vital consideration for every motorcyclist, since a rider's stability and safety depend upon the frictional coefficient of tyres on road. It is surprising how little effort average riders make to recognise road surface dangers in advance, complaining about slipperiness etc after they have had a fright.

Uneven conditions
There should be little to worry about on a clean dry road, but you must always be ready for deterioration in the surface. Potholes and rippled surfaces can be found anywhere, even on quite major roads. Some local authorities spend less than they should on road maintenance programmes, and you will find the quality of the roads worse in some areas than in others. Keep an eye open at road works for loose gravel or wet tar, as both can be lethal. Since passing traffic can spread gravel and chippings some distance away from the area of road works, you may encounter a treacherous surface before you see any warning signs and your first knowledge of it might come when you hear the sound of gravel being flicked up by your bike's tyres.

Slippery surfaces
Besides the obvious dangers in rain, snow, ice or frost, the road can also be made slippery by mud, oil and dust. On the open road always watch for the mud and dust which can gather near a farm entrance or building site. Cobbles or wood-block surfaces in towns require special care, and even asphalt rubbed smooth by sheer weight of traffic demands respect, particularly in wet conditions. Other wet weather hazards include cat's eyes, road studs, manhole covers, drains and sunken gullies. White lines on the road are slippery in wet weather and can cause your bike's front wheel to deviate off course. Battles are still being waged about the pairs of surveying studs often placed right on the two-wheelers' preferred line.

Changing surfaces
The advanced rider constantly looks ahead for changes in the appearance of the road surface. These can take the

form of a different type of surface (perhaps a change from tarmacadam to concrete) or worn areas in a surface. The most common sign is where the dull, coarse appearance of standard surface dressing is broken by shiny, polished patches where the top layer has been worn down to a smooth surface. By using the systematic procedure outlined in Chapter 3, you should never need to indulge in the strong braking or hard acceleration which can cause you to come a cropper on such surfaces. These patches require care at the best of times, but with a little rain or morning dew they become quite lethal.

Oily surfaces
One road surface worry which seems to be increasing is the danger caused by patches of diesel fuel spilled from over-filled lorry tanks. Once your bike's wheels are on this exceedingly slippery layer in a corner, you have virtually no chance of staying on. Apart from areas close to a filling station, pools of oil should also be watched for at any points – bends, roundabouts, junctions – where cornering forces cause fuel to spill.

When a problem patch is spotted, use the systematic method of control to alter your course gradually, and as little as possible, to avoid it. There is no point in taking care to avoid a patch of ice under the shade of a hedge only to stray into the path of a car coming up fast behind.

Selective observation

Being observant is essential to advanced riding, but the refinement of this skill comes in learning to be selective in your observation. When riding in a busy city centre, for example, you need to be able to distinguish what should be acted upon and what can be ignored. These are some pointers to give you an idea of the range of visual information which helps you to become a safer rider:

- Unexpected movements by parked vehicles must always be allowed for (if you see a driver inside). The vehicle can suddenly move out into your path if the driver sets off without thinking, or the driver or a passenger might open a door and step out.

- Telegraph poles changing course can indicate a bend in the road, but remember that occasionally the wires can track straight on while the road bends.
- Cross-winds can blow through gaps between buildings or trees and buffet your machine off its course if you are caught unawares.
- Give stationary tradesmen's vans a wide berth, especially on quiet roads, in case the driver gets out unexpectedly.
- Any parked vehicle can hide a pedestrian about to step out into the road, so it is a good idea to look for tell-tale feet visible from underneath it; school buses and ice cream vans should be treated with particular care.
- Any pedestrian needs to be observed carefully. A child can dash into the road without looking; an old person, perhaps with failing eyesight or hearing, might not see you coming; a dog off a lead could do anything. Be especially careful in wet weather: a pedestrian is not always so careful when he is hurrying for shelter, or if his vision is restricted because he is keeping his head down against the rain.
- Always give a cyclist plenty of room. As a motorcyclist, you should be sensitive to his problems, such as the difficulty of steering a straight course in wind and rain. Not all cyclists are skilled on their machines, so always expect a wobble; a cyclist might also steer round a pothole or drain just as you pass.
- You can glean plenty of information by observing other vehicles. A parked car with its reversing lights on is clearly about to move backwards. A puff from the exhaust of a parked car means that its driver has just started the engine and may pull into your path. A puff from the exhaust of a lorry climbing a hill tells you that its driver has changed down and will be travelling even more slowly; if you are riding down a hill and see a slow-moving lorry climbing towards you, it could conceal a car whose driver is about to attempt a rash overtaking manoeuvre. A decrepit car or van might have poor brakes. Give more room to the sloppy or aggressive driver; drop further back from a driver ahead trying to overtake when there is no

opportunity, or a driver who is paying more attention to finding a particular address in town than he is to the road. If you are behind a bus, a passenger putting his hand up to the bell will give you advance warning that the bus is about to stop.

Stationary vehicles

The advanced rider must pay special attention to stationary and slow-moving cars, particularly at junctions. A TRRL study into the causes of accidents involving motorcycles has revealed that 68 per cent of those resulting in injury occurred at junctions; of these, 73 per cent happened when the motorcycle was travelling straight ahead and a car starting its manoeuvre. Car drivers who fail to see an approaching motorcyclist, or who misjudge its speed, are one of the most frequent and dangerous hazards you must face every time you ride your machine, so look out for them. Careful observation picks up the potentially dangerous car well in advance, so the advanced rider is always able to allow for the driver behaving stupidly.

Road signs

Anyone who has passed the Government test should have all road signs committed to memory, but it is still worth referring to the *Highway Code* periodically to check that you know all the warning signs (triangular), advisory ones (rectangular) and mandatory ones (circular). British roads are quite well provided with signs, and all of them are erected by local authorities for a purpose; you should know at a glance what any sign is telling you. Do not fall into the habit of ignoring signs except when you are searching for particular information, for all of them help in the process of thinking ahead.

Additional observation

No matter how experienced a rider you are, there is always room to improve your observation skills still further. Take pride in developing your own methods. At a familiar junction in town with a restricted view, for example, you might notice that reflections in a shop window act as mirrors and show you what otherwise-invisible traffic is approaching. With this sort of keen observation, the advanced rider can always make his motorcycling that little bit safer.

Summary

- Observation depends upon *good eyesight*, so make sure that you have a sight test frequently (at least every two years) even if you are confident that your vision has not deteriorated.
- *Concentrate your gaze* on a point some way ahead, while at the same time taking in events even further in the distance, closer to you and on either side.
- Use your *mirrors* regularly, but remember that there are many occasions – such as when pulling away from rest or overtaking – when a *glance behind* is also wise.
- Always be watchful for changes in the *road surface* which could reduce the grip of your bike's tyres.
- Develop the skills of *selective observation* so that you have an eye for any situation which might require action from you.

5

POSITIONING

The advanced motorcyclist will always make sure that his machine is correctly positioned on the road. Motorcycles are unable to change direction as quickly as a car, so good positioning – as well as the need to think ahead – is necessary in dealing with hazards and giving the rider the best possible field of vision. Whereas a car driver can respond to an emergency fairly quickly by dodging to left or right, a motorcyclist is less able to take instant evasive action since he can only lean his bike over and change course more gradually at speeds above about 10mph.

Exceptions to the 'keep left' rule

Although the basic rule of the road is that you must keep left except when turning right or overtaking, there are many occasions when a motorcyclist should not keep to the far left-hand side of the road. If he slavishly follows the letter of the law, he will often find himself facing the same difficulties which any driver of a left-hand drive car encounters in Britain – a poor field of vision.

When it is safe to do so, a rider should take up a position which gives him the best view of the road and traffic ahead. This means moving towards the crown of the road (provided that there is no traffic behind) in certain circumstances; for example when approaching an intersection or junction on the left. This temporary position on the road gives the rider an earlier view of vehicles approaching on the adjoining road, since his field of vision across the junction is broader. Equally, it gives any driver waiting to pull out from the side road an earlier view of the approaching motorcycle. Furthermore, a motorcycle which appears to be ridden confidently, well into the road, is more noticeable and seems more important, discouraging drivers from pulling out into the rider's path.

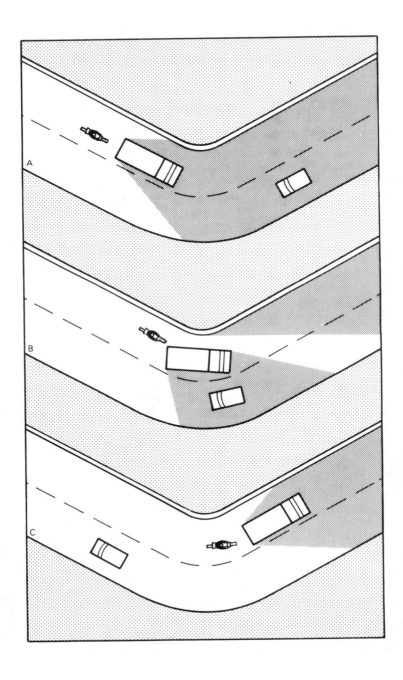

A driver is more likely to think he has time to nip ahead of a motorcycle if it appears to be ridden timidly and against the kerb.

There are many other situations where a position nearer the centre of the road is preferable. Keeping well out when passing parked vehicles gives a better view of approaching hazards such as pedestrian crossings; it allows you to avoid the drains, manhole covers, puddles and loose gravel which can disrupt the road surface near the kerb; and it gives you greater control and vision through bends (as we shall see later). Of course, you must always be careful to check behind you when riding nearer to the centre of the road and be sure that oncoming drivers can see you from a good distance. As we recommend elsewhere in this book, you are safer if you wear 'dayglo' clothing and ride with your headlight illuminated.

It is also important to understand the value of good positioning in relation to other vehicles travelling in your direction. You must never ride too close to a vehicle in front for the obvious reason that you need to be able to stop in the distance available, but it is less widely realised that keeping a good distance gives much better vision. When riding behind a lorry, for example, the best view ahead is available if you hold station even further back than the safe stopping distance. Keeping well back gives earlier warning of junctions on the nearside, parked cars, oncoming traffic, pedestrian crossings and bad patches of road. If the driver behind is not too close, you can broaden your view by moving gently from nearside to offside in your carriageway so that you can see round the vehicle ahead on both sides; if you are the right distance behind this can be done with relatively little change of course.

The importance of correct positioning on the road when following another vehicle, in order to obtain as much forward vision as possible; these are examples of poor positioning. In (A) the rider is approaching the bend with no view around it at all. At the entry to the corner (B) he has missed seeing the approaching car altogether, and his view ahead of the exit (C) is no better.

Positioning on bends

The advanced rider really stands out from the novice in his ability to select the best position when following other vehicles through bends. The accompanying diagrams illustrate the contrast between the unthinking approach and the expert one when following a lorry through a left-hand bend.

The first diagram shows how an inexperienced rider sitting too close to the tail of a lorry might choose a course through a corner. His lack of positioning wisdom means that he can progress through the corner without ever seeing the oncoming car. At first (A) he stays in position close to the lorry's offside, thereby entirely concealing the bend and oncoming traffic. The moment he catches a late glimpse of the bend, he decides to move to the nearside to take a 'straighter' line through the corner, but in doing so he puts the lorry squarely between himself and any vehicles in the bend (B). Coming back to the centre of the road when leaving the bend again cuts down his view past the lorry (C).

The second diagram shows how an advanced rider would tackle the same circumstances. He sits at a safe distance back, gives himself a better view of the road and places himself in just the right position to escape the diesel fumes by overtaking as soon as the road straightens out. He begins his procedure by braking slightly to put more distance between himself and the lorry when the bend approaches, giving himself a chance to look along the nearside of the lorry at oncoming traffic (A). As the lorry begins to turn, he moves towards the centre of the road (B), giving himself a wider view around the curve past the nearside of the lorry while at the same time allowing him to see the oncoming car earlier. He then leans into the corner to take the bend near its apex, maintaining his view along the truck's nearside so that he can see a good distance up

By keeping further behind the lorry and taking the right line around the bend, the rider has a view of approaching traffic all the way through, and can see the left-hand pavement on the exit.

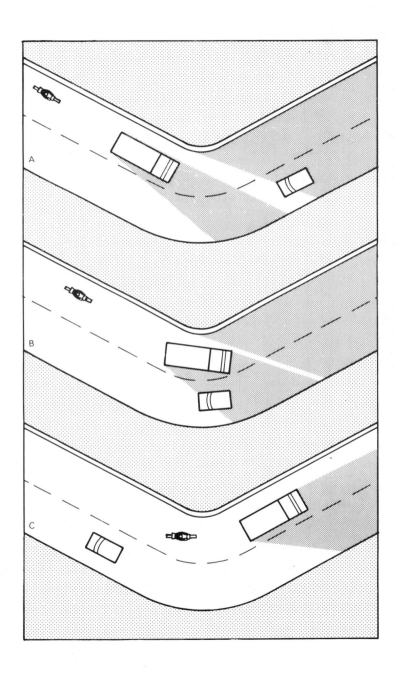

the straight stretch of road ahead (C). Although the lorry still obscures part of the road, he knows from his earlier nearside observation that this section is clear. He is well positioned, therefore, to accelerate smoothly out of the bend and move across his side of the road again ready to overtake the lorry if it is safe to do so.

The ideal line for a right-hand bend is the one which an advanced rider would take if the road were empty: in other words, he should keep to the left on approach for a wider view through the bend, move towards the centre line through the bend to 'straighten' it (after checking his mirror and without crossing the line, of course) and then edge back to the centre for the earliest view up the straight stretch which follows. Straightening the bend in this way gives a safer, shallower and more even arc through the turn, leaving the rider in a good position if there is an opportunity to overtake.

Right-hand bends can present good opportunities for preparing an overtaking manoeuvre because the road ahead is visible early on. An advanced rider, however, never moves so close to the crown of the road at the apex that he alarms oncoming drivers, and always makes sure that there are no cars close behind before altering his position on the road. If another road user is immediately behind and possibly considering a foolish overtaking manoeuvre, it is better to stay on the nearside.

Although we shall meet the subject of positioning frequently during the course of this book, one last word is appropriate now. When approaching junctions with 'stop' signs, traffic lights, filter lights or lanes marked for taking a left or right turn, you should take up a position in the centre of the appropriate lane well in advance. Not only does this help motorists to notice you, but it also means that they are less likely to force you out of the lane by pulling close alongside. Even if your lane dictates your path through the junction, it is still best to signal in order to reinforce your intentions.

Summary

- Always be aware of the need for *good positioning* on the road so that you have the best possible field of vision.
- As long as it is safe to do so, do not hesitate to move towards the *crown of the road* if this gives you a better view of approaching hazards or a smoother surface to ride upon: parked vehicles, nearside junctions and stretches of poor surface near the kerb are all occasions when this practice can be advisable.
- *Positioning on a bend* should be judged so that you maximise vision around vehicles ahead and take the turn with a shallow arc.

6

CORNERING

Many accidents involving motorcycles occur on bends and corners, and when these happen on an empty road there is no-one to blame except the rider himself. Every time a motorcycle follows a curved course, rider and machine are engaged in a delicate balancing act which can easily be upset. Handling a motorcycle sensitively and competently through corners is essential to a rider's safety, but the necessary level of skill is acquired only with experience. As a result, the advanced rider must apply the general principles repeatedly until smooth, safe cornering becomes almost instinctive.

Cornering forces

It is worth analysing the forces which act on a motorcycle when it is directed round a corner. Unlike cars, motorcycles are not steered through corners except at very low speeds or when parking. Instead, the rider makes a turn by banking over so that the weight of rider and machine act against the natural momentum which takes the moving mass in a straight line. This sideways force makes the machine start to turn, while centrifugal force acts in the opposite direction to stop the bike from toppling over. Every time a motorcycle goes through a corner there is a balance between the main forces: the weight of rider and bike banked over, the centrifugal force pulling the bike towards the outside of the turn and the frictional resistance of the tyres on the road surface.

Centrifugal force tries to push the motorcycle outwards in the same way that a piece of string with a weight at the end tautens when you swing it through the air. The faster you whirl a weighted string, the greater the centrifugal force; in the same way a bike is pulled more strongly away from its intended course the faster it is

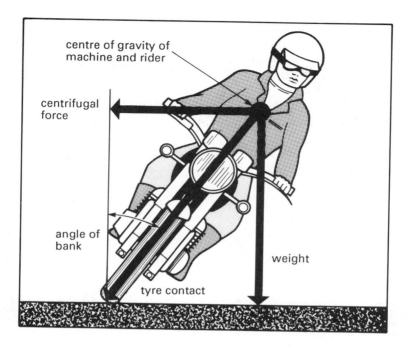

centre of gravity of
machine and rider

centrifugal
force

angle of
bank

weight

tyre contact

Cornering: the rider instinctively leans into the bend. Centrifugal force counteracts the pull of gravity – and tyre grip becomes all-important.

This is all well and good, except that this balance can always be upset by any sudden change in these forces. There are three usual causes of this balance being destroyed. First, the frictional resistance of your tyres can be changed if the road surface alters or the tyres cannot provide the adhesion the rider demands. Second, a patch of bumpy road can cause the suspension to oscillate and break tyre adhesion, although the handling qualities of modern bikes have helped to reduce this danger. Third, excessive speed can increase the centrifugal force to the point where it is impossible to lean the bike over any further to compensate.

In the first case, the tyres start to skid, which can lead to the banked weight pulling the bike to the ground. In the second, the oscillations can build up until one force overcomes the others and the bike crashes. In the third, centrifugal force pulls the bike so hard towards a straighter course that the rider runs off the outside of the bend. Of course, judging the speed appropriate for the conditions – taking into account visibility, the condition of the surface and the tightness of the bend – is the secret of avoiding any of these alarming situations.

Control through bends

Great care must be taken to minimise accelerating or braking on a bend: acceleration increases centrifugal force and braking increases the loading on the tyres to the point where a skid can occur. The key to avoiding any risk on corners is to keep the forces well under the limits where the balance can be destroyed, which simply means riding at a restrained speed.

By taking a corner at a sensible speed, centrifugal force remains low, the bike does not have to be banked far over, and the tyres have plenty of frictional reserves in hand in case you meet a patch of slippery road. The golden rule is simple: take every bend at a speed which does not call for excessive banking. A smooth course through a bend at steady speed will prevent any sudden alteration of the forces acting on your bike; lifting the bike a little or banking it further may be necessary through a bend of changing radius, but can only be regarded as safe when there is no other change in the forces involved. Only at very slow speeds should you ever brake or accelerate in a bend, unless this is essential in an emergency. Going through a bend on a trailing throttle or changing down a gear can also bring about a dangerous change in the balance of forces. Remember, too, that some front brakes cause the machine to sit up when applied firmly. In the final part of a bend moderate acceleration is permissible, since this helps to pull the bike upright again when centrifugal force is increased.

While these observations are applicable to all bends,

there are certain differences, as the advanced rider will appreciate, for left-hand and right-hand bends. Road camber is the most important: through a left-hander it improves the angle of contact between tyre and road surface, but through a righter-hander it worsens the angle. In effect, this means that right-hand bends have to be taken slightly more slowly than left-handers, although good positioning – if conditions allow the correct line to be followed – can help to minimise the effect of adverse camber on right-handers.

Positioning on bends

Considerations of safety, road surface, other road users and visibility all affect your decision about how much of the width of your carriageway you use when negotiating a bend, since the best course means optimising your position on the road. However, you can use the procedure which follows surprisingly often.

Left-hand

For left-hand bends (see the accompanying diagram), you can obtain the best view around the corner by taking up a position towards the centre of the road, after checking your mirrors and adjusting your speed. You then check again to make sure that nothing is coming up on the nearside from behind, and sweep smoothly in towards the kerb so that you come closest to it just after the apex. From this point, you can use a little more of the road to continue the process of flattening the curve, thereby making it less acute. Of course, you should always be certain that it is safe to take this course; if you are in any doubt you should hold the nearside all the way through. Riding in dense traffic, approaching roadworks, taking account of a poor road surface or seeing skid marks on the road are all occasions when you should slow down and keep firmly to the nearside until a clear view forwards can be obtained.

Right-hand

For right-hand bends (see the second diagram), maximising your view of the road ahead means that you approach on the nearside and then choose a gradual curve

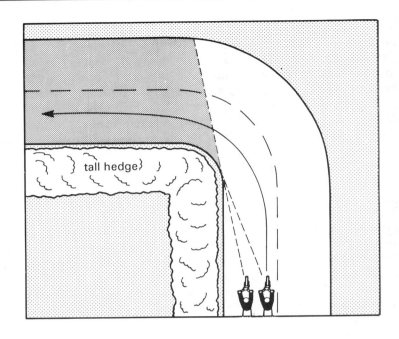

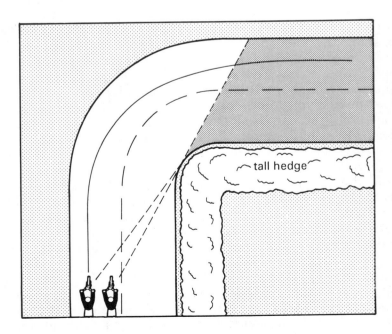

towards the centre as soon as you can see through the corner. This point will occur sooner on an open bend than on one bounded by tall hedges or walls. As well as improving your view, this more gradual course gives your bike's tyres better grip since they do not have to cope with so much adverse camber at the apex of the bend. You can accelerate slightly – as long as the road is dry and the surface good – after you pass the apex to help your bike back to a nearside course, following a glance in the mirrors to check the traffic behind.

Emergency action

You must remember two facts about your machine's behaviour when faced with an emergency, such as someone else having an accident in front of you on a bend. Acceleration will tend to push the bike wide, while lifting off or braking will tend to tighten its line; doing either in excess will cause a tyre to skid and possibly cause you to have an accident too.

Once the inexperienced rider is aware of the dangers of upsetting the balance of forces acting on his machine through a bend, he will be able to develop his skills so that he can corner quite safely at steady speeds. With practice and experience, smooth, safe cornering can be one of the most pleasurable aspects of motorcycling.

Summary

- Corners should be taken *smoothly and at constant speed*, without excessive banking, to avoid upsetting the delicate balance of forces involved.
- Avoid *acceleration or braking* on a bend (except at very slow speeds), unless it is essential in an emergency. Moderate acceleration through the final

Correct positioning on bends is important not only from the point of view of taking the bend itself – by following the right line the rider in these diagrams gets the maximum view around the curve and will spot any hazard on the exit all the sooner.

part of a bend is permissible to transfer more of the bike's weight to the back wheel, thus improving adhesion.

● When road and traffic conditions allow, adjust your *position on the road* through a corner, using the methods outlined for left-hand and right-hand bends, to flatten a curve and give yourself a better view through it.

7

BRAKING IN WET AND DRY CONDITIONS

Considerable sensitivity and skill is required when slowing down a motorcycle by using the brakes. When conditions are difficult – such as in bad weather, on a poor surface or when fierce braking is called for in an emergency – the slightest mistake in braking can quickly develop into a fall, or even a serious accident. Braking can be carried out smoothly and safely if the correct methods are always applied with proper regard for road and traffic conditions.

Use of front and rear brakes

The advanced rider will understand the finer points of using the front and rear brakes. Braking always causes the combined weight of rider and machine to be thrown forward so that the front tyre is forced more strongly against the road. On a dry and even surface this weight transfer usefully increases the front tyre's grip and makes the front brake more effective, but on a wet or poor surface it significantly increases the chances of a front wheel skid. At the same time, the corresponding reduction in weight on the rear wheel makes this more likely to lock up too. A locked wheel is not only completely useless as a brake, but it also removes the rider's control of his machine until he releases pressure on the brake to get the wheel turning again.

Poor road conditions

From experience the advanced rider learns how braking effort should be distributed between front and rear wheels. On a dry road he tends to put around 75 per cent of the braking effort on to the front wheel and around 25 per cent on to the rear wheel, but this distribution must be adjusted when conditions are not perfect. When a good surface is wet about 50 per cent should go to each wheel, but in worse conditions – such as when a surface is loose or icy, or affected by wet leaves, mud or oil – the rear brake only should be used, taking care to avoid locking the wheel. On such surfaces the more powerful front brake, helped by weight transfer, can lock very easily. Worse still, if road camber or uneven weight distribution causes the skidding front wheel to slide to one side while it is locked, an accident is almost inevitable.

Consideration of the road surface is far more vital for a motorcyclist than a car driver, so constant assessment must be made of how much to use the lever for front braking and foot pedal for rear braking. In good conditions the front brake does most of the work, balanced and complemented by the rear brake. All the time, the rider thinks ahead so that he can apply the brakes early, use gentle pressure to avoid danger and minimise brake wear, and leave a good margin of braking power and distance so that he can cope with any surprises. All these factors hold good regardless of the circumstances, but in poorer weather and surface conditions he makes less use of the front brake. On very slippery or uneven roads most of your retardation should be achieved by engine braking/correct gear selection so that when speed is sufficiently reduced only the rear brake need be used.

If you do lock either wheel when braking, you need to release the pressure momentarily to allow the locked wheel to turn again, and then reapply the brake more gently. Maximum braking effort is achieved at the point just before a wheel locks, but motorcyclists must leave a good margin because of the loss of control which results when a wheel does lock.

Choosing your braking surface

It may seem a commonsense observation, but it is worth

remembering to select a good patch of road for braking whenever possible, and allow a margin for road surface changes when judging your braking. If you spot a shiny section of asphalt leading into a bend, plan your braking so that your speed is reduced before you reach it. Ease off the pressure momentarily if you find the surface deteriorating under your wheels. While this seems quite obvious, a surprising number of riders seem to press on regardless of road surface, only to find that they need to resort to wild body contortions just to stay upright when the bike starts to slide.

Smooth braking

By applying the skills of advanced motorcycling, it should seldom be necessary to brake fiercely. Braking should always be smooth and progressive, and you should leave a good margin in case heavier braking becomes necessary. When braking to a halt, the best procedure is to apply the brakes smoothly for two-thirds to three-quarters of the distance in which you wish to stop, easing up on the pressure for the last one-third to a quarter. Gentle braking for the last section gives you a margin if you have miscalculated or need to stop sooner than you expect, perhaps if the man ahead pulls up short of the 'stop' line.

Use lower gears as well as the brakes when riding downhill or on slippery surfaces and try to check your speed adequately before each turn so that your braking can be carried out in a straight line, remembering also to allow for your speed increasing again as you ride through a descending bend.

Braking distance

Just as important as an appreciation of braking methods is an understanding of the distance needed to stop a motorcycle from any speed. Many riders leave a distance which is adequate only if the vehicle in front slows down at a normal rate, but just occasionally it stops a good deal quicker if it hits another vehicle ahead. The safe distance is one in which you can come to a complete stop in an emergency.

The safe distance is the sum of braking *and* thinking

distance. While it is true that a motorcyclist should be able to react in an emergency more quickly than a car driver since the hand and foot are already in position over the brakes, the reaction time needed for the brain to assess a situation and send its message must be considered. Someone who can do this in 0.5 second has superb reactions, yet in this time a motorcycle travelling at 30mph moves 22 feet before the brakes go on, and then at least another 30 feet are needed to stop in good conditions. To ride safely at 30mph, therefore, you must allow an absolute minimum of 52 feet between you and the vehicle in front. Many people's reactions are not as quick as 0.5 second, and, if hands and feet are cold, reaction times become even longer: the space needed to stop from 30mph goes up to 74 feet for someone with a reaction time of 1 second. What all this amounts to is that thinking distance is a significant figure to be added to the actual braking distance.

Braking distances do not increase directly in proportion with speed; double the speed to 60mph and you should leave at least 180 feet for an emergency stop. A rough rule of thumb is to square the speed and divide by 20 (for 60mph, for example, $60 \times 60 = 3600 \div 20 = 180$ feet), but this is not really practicable. The advanced rider judges safety by using road-craft rather than filling his head with odd sums which cannot possibly cope with fast-changing road and traffic conditions.

Braking on a bend

It is advisable to brake only when the machine is upright and travelling in a straight line, varying the pressure and front-rear distribution according to road surface conditions. By thinking ahead, as outlined in Chapter 2, the advanced rider can plan his actions so that braking should never be needed on a corner.

Just occasionally, however, even the most expert rider will be faced with an emergency which leaves him with no choice but to brake while the bike is banked over in a bend. In these circumstances, you must remember that excessive use of the brakes will upset the balance of forces and throw one or both wheels into a skid, making a fall virtually inevitable. Of course, the emergency may be so extreme that you need to stop as sharply as possible with both brakes, and it could be that losing control and taking your chances with the road surface seems less catastrophic than hitting an unforeseen stationary obstruction.

It must be emphasised again that the advanced rider chooses a speed appropriate to his field of vision when entering a corner so that he can allow for emergency action. He should not rely on braking ability once his bike is banked over.

Discs and drums

The main advantage of the disc brake is its resistance to fade, and therefore its ability to stop a heavy bike repeatedly from high speed, or to cope with the demands of a series of hairpin bends on the descent from a mountain pass. On the other hand, discs tend to require more pressure at low speeds and do not always perform as well in wet weather.

When discs were first offered on motorcycles, the general view was that aesthetic appeal and imitation of racing practice were the main selling points. Most Japanese machines were equipped with stainless steel discs, and with the then state of knowledge about friction pad materials their wet-weather braking characteristics were appalling. One or two European manufacturers followed car industry practice in using cast-iron discs which gave better braking in the wet, but the layer of rust which formed whenever the bike was left standing for more than a few hours was considered unsightly.

Thankfully, the friction pad technicians took a hand in the scene and produced sintered metal products which could give tolerably good retardation even on stainless steel discs. Interim solutions included drilling or incorporating slots in the discs: although this became general practice, some manufacturers reverted to solid discs for rear brakes to eliminate distortion and cracks caused by overheating.

Happily the situation has improved dramatically, to the point where the latest disc designs offer superb braking under all conditions. In fact, on the majority of Japanese superbikes the front brakes are bordering on the over-sensitive, making it possible to lock up the front wheel on a dry road with only light finger pressure. The skilled rider can use the tremendous power which these brakes offer, but for most levels of competence something else is needed.

That something else – anti-lock braking – is now commonly available to the car driver, and there are numerous signs that the motorcycle manufacturers are following the same route. From the first days of anti-lock car brakes, experiments began with similar brakes for two-wheelers although early designs were cumbersome. They gave an unacceptable penalty in unsprung weight, and the fact that they were mechanically actuated meant that a lot of design sorting was needed before they could be mass-produced.

The advent of on-board computers and microchip technology on the automotive scene meant that electronic controls could be used, and BMW's Anti-lock Braking System (ABS) was the first in the world to be offered for motorcycles. It is expensive, but seems to be the answer in all other respects. Those who have tested BMW's ABS invariably comment about how hard the brakes can be applied before they come into action. So far ABS has been available only to experienced riders who can afford the best machinery, but novice riders stand to benefit much more once ABS becomes affordable. Alternatives, including an elegant mechanical system from Girling, are under development, and the Japanese cannot be long in emulating BMW.

For conventional braking systems, however, a few closing comments are appropriate. It is important to become familiar with the braking characteristics of any machine when you ride it for the first time. Different motorcycle makes and models vary considerably in the way they handle under braking, and the condition of tyres, pads, discs, linings, drums and controls all affect braking behaviour. Make a point, therefore, of trying out the brakes on a quiet stretch of good road by stopping firmly from 30mph with about 75 per cent front and 25 per cent rear distribution. What you learn about the bike's feel under braking in safe conditions could be very useful if you face an emergency before you are thoroughly familiar with the machine.

It is good practice to give each brake a dab soon after starting every journey, no matter how short, to make sure that the brakes are working well. A quick visual check over the brakes before every journey is also wise, as you may spot frayed cable ends, worn cable casings or leaks from hydraulic pipes. Brake adjustment, of course, is an important part of a motorcycle's regular maintenance needs.

Summary

- Understand the fine points of using *front and rear brakes*. Normal conditions require about 75 per cent of braking effort on the front wheel, but wet or poor road surfaces require more use of the rear brake. When the road is very slippery, use engine braking and the rear brake.

- Always be aware of the *braking distance* you need at any speed, and allow for *thinking distance* too in your safety margin.

- Remember that recommended braking distances are for good conditions and straight-line braking: on *wet or bad roads* leave even more room.

8

GEARCHANGING

Using the gearbox correctly is not only essential to riding safely but it also reduces the mechanical wear and tear on engine and transmission. There is one basic principle which the advanced rider follows: he will always be travelling at the right speed for the conditions and with the correct gear engaged. Good use of the gearbox has to be developed with experience, to the point where the advanced rider has an almost instinctive knack for knowing which gear will produce the best response from his motorcycle in any circumstances.

Use of the gearbox

A gearbox is necessary so that an engine can work within its comfortable operating range whether going up a steep hill or along a level road, whether at 5mph or 70mph. A three-speed or four-speed gearbox used to be sufficient to transmit power from an engine which delivered good torque at relatively low revs, but the trend of many modern designs, particularly some of the sophisticated two-strokes from Japanese manufacturers, is towards more high-revving engines (some capable of more than 10,000rpm) with narrow power bands which require five-speed or even six-speed gearboxes. The need to pay attention to correct gear selection before it is required is necessary on any bike, but on a machine such as this, with little throttle response outside its tight power band, correct gear selection becomes even more important.

Even experienced riders can be guilty of some of these common gearchanging faults: staying in top gear for too long so that a down-change is forced upon the rider when the engine starts to labour; moving away in second gear and slipping the clutch unnecessarily; and running up and down the gears so excessively that the engine spends much of its time revving hard and wearing itself out. The aim of the advanced rider is to keep the engine within its comfortable operating range so that it is neither labouring nor racing too fast, and to prepare himself for any hazard by selecting a lower gear – for better acceleration or braking – well in advance.

Using the rev counter
The rev counters fitted as standard equipment to many motorcycles can be a useful aid to gearchanging, particularly on those high-revving machines with narrow power bands. While the advanced rider should be completely familiar with his machine's abilities, referring to the rev counter can help his decisions about when to change gear. He will learn with experience which segment of the rev band produces the strongest acceleration, but the rev counter can also remind him to change up to reduce revs and improve economy when travelling at a steady speed. The rev counter's other purpose is to indicate maximum engine revs: no safe rider habitually uses all the power available to him but there are occasions, such as during overtaking, when it may be necessary to take the engine close to its red-lined maximum. But remember that the red line marks the maximum revs the manufacturer recommends, and not necessarily the point at which it produces its maximum power; taking the engine all the way to the red line will not generally produce any performance advantage. Machines fitted with electronic ignition controls often incorporate an ignition cut-out to prevent over-revving, and at least one design cuts out two of the four sparks as the danger point is reached.

If your machine does not have a rev counter, it would be useful to find out from the manufacturer's handbook the maximum speeds permissible in each gear and perhaps mark them on the speedometer as a precaution against accidental over-revving. While the advanced rider should always know which gear he is in, the digital indicators of gear selected (as well as a neutral light) fitted to many bikes can be beneficial when getting to know a new or unfamiliar machine, especially if it has a six-speed gearbox. With today's gearing for performance, with close-ratio gears allied to multi-cylinder power units, the digital gear indicator can no longer be criticised as an 'idiot light'.

Slowing down

Using the gears

When changing to a lower gear, you should use sufficient throttle to match engine speed with road speed when you release the clutch, this procedure requiring careful judgement so that the change is as smooth as possible. Smooth clutch action and a balanced throttle are especially important in slippery conditions, since closing the throttle and releasing the clutch sharply are as likely to cause the rear wheel to skid as applying the brakes suddenly.

Although the efficiency of modern car brakes means that drivers are no longer recommended to use the gearbox as an aid to slowing down, intelligent use of the gearbox's braking effect is an integral part of motorcycling. Using the gears to slow down your machine is particularly valuable on wet and slippery surfaces as the engine, on closed throttle, gives a gentle braking effect which is less likely to lock the rear wheel than using the brake alone. On a good surface a combination of engine braking and brakes is used for gradual slowing down, but the engine can play a greater part the worse the conditions get, so that on ice or loose gravel the brake can be ignored except for coming to a final halt.

How you fit this advice to circumstances depends entirely on how much the speed of your machine needs to be reduced when approaching a hazard. Sometimes use of the gears alone will do, but if you judge that the brakes are needed they should be used first, followed by the gearchanging necessary for added braking or subsequent acceleration.

Using neutral

Finding neutral in a motorcycle's gearbox used to be an exercise requiring sensitive foot control and concentration, but nowadays better selector design (and electric light indicators) make the task easier. The advanced rider selects neutral only when virtually at a standstill; and then he will *always* do it when at rest for any appreciable time, to avoid wearing out the clutch components and actuating mechanism by running the engine with first gear engaged while waiting to move off again. A useful pointer to an inexperienced motorcyclist is the tendency to hold the clutch lever in the withdrawn position against the handlebar for long periods while waiting to move off.

Some riders develop the dangerous habit of selecting neutral some time before they stop, perhaps when approaching traffic lights or a junction, and coasting to a halt. To do so breaks the fundamental rule of always being in the right gear at the right time, leaving the rider unable to accelerate away from unexpected danger and denied of the valuable engine braking effect. He could find himself having to engage a gear very quickly in an emergency, which could result in letting out the clutch lever with the engine revving excessively – a mistake which could cause a rear wheel skid in extreme circumstances. For the same reason it is important not to change down to a lower gear too early when slowing down or planning brisk acceleration, as the engine could run past its limit and the action of releasing the clutch could create dangerous instability.

Acceleration

Just as much care must be taken when accelerating up through the gears, as insensitive use of the clutch and throttle can cause the rear wheel to break traction briefly; this can be induced very easily on a powerful motorcycle, and makes the machine difficult to control when it occurs. Every motorcyclist must learn to use wisely the acceleration available to him, leaving a good safety margin and observing the road surface carefully.

Particular care is needed when starting from rest, when the lower gears on all but the smallest machines give more rapid acceleration than on most cars; every rider must be familiar with the temptation to prove this. Apart from the dangers of spinning the rear wheel on a slippery surface, excessive acceleration can cause a loss of control resulting from the front wheel lifting up from the road surface in a 'wheelie'. Weight transfer to the rear combined with strong power driving the rear wheel forwards creates this situation, and the effect is felt in light steering before the front wheel actually leaves the ground.

Although the 'wheelie' is part of the racer's repertoire on the circuit these days, on the road such behaviour impresses no one and is courting danger unnecessarily. It should be avoided by using the throttle progressively and changing gear smoothly. Acceleration can be quite rapid enough within these margins, but it should always be safe for the prevailing road and traffic conditions.

Summary

- There is a basic principle about the *use of gears*; always travel at the *right speed* with the *right gear* engaged to cope with any conditions.
- Gearchanges should be made *smoothly and precisely*; smooth downward changes require the appropriate twist grip position to match engine speed to road speed when drive takes up again.
- As well as the brakes, the gearbox can be used to *slow down* your machine; the use of engine compression to lose speed is safer on *slippery roads* than braking.
- Learn the *maximum road speed* possible in the lower gears, with the help of the rev counter if your motorcycle has one.

9

OVERTAKING

One of the great advantages of owning a motorcycle is that it can allow you to make quicker journeys than other traffic over congested roads. A motorcycle's small dimensions enable it to pass long rows of slow-moving vehicles on busy trunk roads, while every motorcyclist who rides regularly in towns and cities knows the pleasure of being able to move quietly to the front of any queue at traffic lights and junctions. Even on quieter roads, the relative ease of overtaking slower vehicles is another advantage for the motorcyclist. Any overtaking manoeuvre, however, is potentially dangerous, requiring all the skill, judgement, concentration and knowledge the rider can muster.

When to overtake

Even on an ordinary road, overtaking requires careful planning, rapid thinking and decisiveness. If the width of the road means that you have to cross the broken centre line in order to make your move, you must be certain that the road is clear far enough ahead to allow you to pull out, accelerate, overtake and pull back in again without alarming an oncoming driver in the distance, or forcing the driver you are passing to take action to help you out of a sticky situation. Overtaking can take a considerable time on a motorcycle of modest power, even if you use all the acceleration available to you. If an approaching vehicle comes into sight over a brow or round a bend while you are still making your manoeuvre, you could be in trouble – and you will scare the drivers around you.

Overtaking speed
When judging distances before overtaking, take into account the huge difference between overtaking and

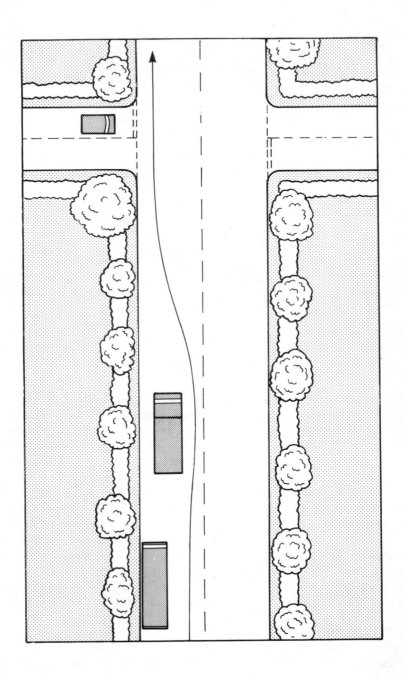

closing speeds. Overtaking a car travelling at 45mph when you are doing 60mph means that you will pass it at a cyclist's pace, but the lorry coming the other way may also be doing 60mph, giving a closing speed with you of 120mph. That means the lorry closes with you by almost 180 feet every second, so you must be in the right position with the correct gear selected to be past the car in front well before you are caught between the two. You *must not* make mistakes when you overtake: if in doubt hold back.

Hidden hazards

Besides assessing whether there is time to overtake safely, the operation must be planned with great care, not with the air of optimism which a few irresponsible riders employ. As well as allowing for oncoming vehicles, you must also be prepared for the driver who might come out of a side turning, drive or lay-by. He may pause at the main road, look to his right to check that nothing is coming on his side of the road and then pull out; it might never occur to him that an overtaking motorcycle or car could be approaching from the left. This potentially dangerous scenario happens all too frequently, and you should not consider an overtaking manoeuvre on the approach to a side turning, drive or lay-by.

Correct application of road-craft will allow you to anticipate danger from a concealed drive or unsignposted

Overtaking: the rider whose path is shown in the diagram has pulled out to pass the stationary bus, then overtaken the truck while still keeping to the left of the white line. But a manoeuvre like this with a crossroads coming up can be fraught with potential danger: the truck driver may be about to turn off but is not bothering to signal (or is unaware of the fact that his indicator is not working). The car waiting to pull out from the side road represents another danger: the driver may not have seen our rider, obscured as the motorcycle will be for him by the oncoming truck. The motorist may decide he has time to pull out in front of the truck, never dreaming that a motorcycle is bearing down on him along the middle of the road.

lane, and you will be ready to sound the horn or flash the headlight to draw attention to yourself if a vehicle appears.

Overtaking technique

Once you have satisfied yourself that there is plenty of room for you to overtake safely, you should check your mirrors and/or glance behind before starting your move. To make sure that you have a good view of the conditions ahead you should take up a position near the centre of the road and hang far enough back so that you can see well past the offside of the vehicle ahead. You must be certain that no hazards are approaching and that there is a suitable gap ahead for you to pull in again safely. Normally there is room for you to complete the manoeuvre, but just occasionally a large lorry can be following other traffic so closely that you could embark on a manoeuvre only to find that you have to pass two or three vehicles in one go, not one.

Procedure
If there is no-one behind you who is about to overtake and no-one already coming up on the outside (and possibly only visible to you with a proper glance behind), give a right-turn signal, change down to a lower gear for stronger acceleration if necessary, and apply power firmly but smoothly as you move out on to a path well clear of the vehicle in front. The gear you choose will ideally get you through to the completion of your manoeuvre before the engine revs reach the point where you need to change up. As you approach the rear of the vehicle you plan to pass, you will have a useful opportunity to check the road in front on the nearside – an area which may have been hidden from your view earlier. Clearly you will have to postpone your manoeuvre if you see any hazards which will cause the driver in front to change course.

Awareness
Once you are making your manoeuvre, keep a careful eye out for any signs that the driver ahead might change

course for no apparent reason, or even suddenly decide to overtake the vehicle in front of him or turn right. It is essential to watch him carefully, making quite sure he has seen you and knows your intention to pass; sometimes he may courteously move towards the nearside to give you more room, but it is more than a slim possibility that he will move towards you without checking in his mirror or signalling. An illuminated headlight, bright clothing and a reflective belt all help to attract attention. If he starts to move, or even if you suspect that he might, use the horn to warn him of your presence. Try to use the horn with the suggestion of politeness which short notes can convey, as far too many drivers interpret the sound of a horn as an insult or even a challenge. This practice is used frequently on the continent, and ought to be used more willingly by motorcyclists and drivers in Britain.

The awkward driver

Some car drivers seem to resent being overtaken and behave quite insanely. They may even close the gap ahead of them to shut you out in the right-hand lane or accelerate while you are passing. Always keep your anger under control and resist any temptation to retaliate, either by trying to race the driver or by squeezing into the shrinking gap ahead of him; two angry people are twice as dangerous as one, and you will come off far worse than the car driver. Treat such stupid behaviour in the only sensible way, by pulling back into place behind the car.

Bad weather conditions

Overtaking is obviously even more dangerous in bad conditions: the road surface is more treacherous, and spray thrown up by traffic makes visibility poor. Since visibility is worst just at the point where you are most vulnerable, close up behind the vehicle in front on an overtaking course, remember that the reasonable view ahead available when you were lying back waiting to overtake can be obscured by a cloud of spray as you make your manoeuvre.

Courtesy and consideration

When traffic is heavy, a motorcyclist can usually make his way past long strings of slow-moving or stationary vehicles, and free himself from some of the frustrating delay which car drivers must tolerate. It is vital that this process is done safely and courteously, and the rider must constantly be alert to the possibility of pedestrians and cars suddenly appearing through gaps in the traffic. Speed must be kept right down to allow for other road users crossing what seems to them to be a row of stationary vehicles, and perhaps not even looking your way. You must also watch for drivers pulling out of a line of slow-moving or stationary traffic in order to turn right or even make a U-turn; they might well do so without checking behind because they assume that all the traffic behind has stopped too, completely forgetting about the existence of motorcycles. All this means that the motorcyclist must proceed past a line of vehicles very slowly, with the utmost care and preferably on the offside. If you are passing a jam with a view to turning left at a junction, it is permissible to make careful use of the clear space on the nearside.

Summary

- Ensure that you always overtake *safely*, when there is plenty of time available to complete the manoeuvre. Do not overtake if you would have to pass a *side turning* or *pedestrian crossing* while doing so.
- *Overtaking procedure*: check your mirror, glance behind and signal before moving out; engage a lower gear if necessary and accelerate firmly but smoothly; do not cut in sharply at the end of the manoeuvre; be prepared for foolish behaviour or ignorance of your presence from the driver you are passing.
- Take the utmost care when passing a row of *slow-moving or stationary traffic*, and do so on the offside unless you plan to turn left; be prepared for drivers who consider it unnecessary to check behind before pulling out of the stream to make a turn.

10

JUNCTIONS

Extra risks face motorcyclists wherever roads meet and converge, whether at crossroads, T-junctions, roundabouts or forks. A study by the Transport and Road Research Laboratory has shown that 78 per cent of motorcycle accidents causing personal injury involved other vehicles, and that 68 per cent of these occurred at junctions or roundabouts. Accidents do not 'just happen' of their own accord – they are caused by the mistakes made by all road users. By using the techniques of advanced motorcycling and applying a systematic approach, junctions can be dealt with as safely as any other part of the road system. However, while you should always take extra care at junctions, you must recognise that they present an ideal opportunity for other road users to cause trouble, particularly for the motorcyclist. We have all seen drivers adopt their own odd ways of approaching junctions and navigating their way through them. Be on your guard, therefore, for what a road safety expert might describe as 'an accident waiting to happen'.

Crossroads

Most opportunities for error, whether on your part or on the part of another road user, occur at crossroads. When you are approaching on the minor route, or when neither route has precedence, brake and change down so that you are ready to stop (even though the signs may tell you only to give way) and pay attention to your positioning. If your side of the road is wide enough for two lanes of traffic, ensure that you start moving into the correct one at an early stage after first checking your mirror and signalling accordingly if necessary.

Straight on or left turn

Stay in the nearside of the left-hand lane if you intend to go straight across or turn left, unless lane markings tell you to do otherwise; take the right-hand lane if you intend to turn right. Even if there is insufficient room for doubling up the traffic lanes, it is still better to move to the side corresponding with the route you will follow as you leave the junction. When planning to go straight ahead or turning left, the procedure is relatively simple: wait until the road is clear to right and left, check that nothing is approaching from the opposite minor road and accelerate smartly away. Always watch, however, for one common cause of accidents. An oncoming vehicle signalling to turn left will lead you to expect it to turn off at the crossroads and not interfere with your intended path, but indicators can be left on by mistake. Never assume that the vehicle will turn until you actually see the driver begin moving into another road. The only *reliable* information obtained from a flashing indicator is that the bulb is working!

Right turn

Right turns at crossroads can be more complicated because of the confusion which arises with opposing traffic also waiting to turn right. Half of the country's drivers seem to favour passing offside-to-offside, the other half the other way. However, the usual rule is to pass offside-to-offside; in other words, pass behind an opposing vehicle waiting to turn right. Do otherwise only when road markings or the junction layout dictate it. Passing round behind other traffic gives you a clear view ahead as you make your turn, whereas the nearside-to-nearside approach forces drivers and riders to nose out blindly across the traffic stream, increasing the chances of a collision. It is hardly surprising that so many accidents

Correct and incorrect procedure when turning right at a junction. Unless lane markings or police directions instruct otherwise, you should turn offside-to-offside, as in the picture above. In the picture below the rider and the driver are obstructing one another's view of approaching traffic.

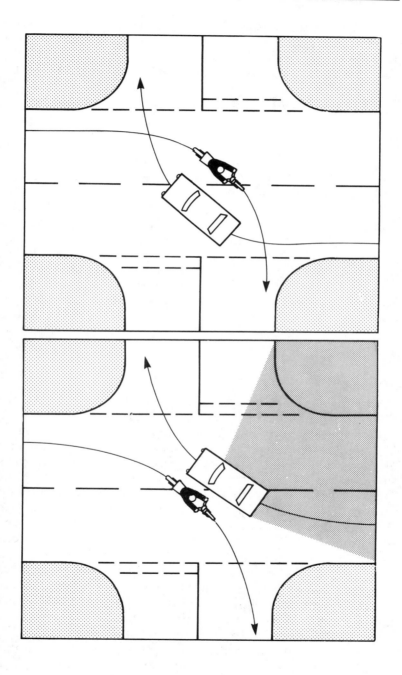

occur where traffic turns right. Just because you have a clearer and relatively higher view from your motorcycle than most car drivers, never be tempted to cut across a junction in a way which other road users will not be expecting in order to nip through ahead of a stream of traffic; make your turn safely behind another right-turning driver.

Safety rather than assertion
Using the more major of the two routes at a crossroads does not entitle you to ride as you like. A driver may still make an unsignalled, sudden turn in front of you or he may slow down abruptly; there is also a very real chance that someone waiting to pull out from a side road will do so in front of you. Show courtesy and consideration to other road users, but not so excessively that you put politeness before practicality. By all means let someone out of a side turning if it is safe for you to do so, but it is foolish if you have to cause drivers behind you to brake. Misplaced courtesy can cause problems for other road users who are not expecting it.

Traffic lights

Never take advantage of traffic light changes to try to nip through a junction and save yourself time; trying rashly to save a few seconds puts yourself and pedestrians at risk. You should stop if you can reasonably do so when green changes to amber, and you must certainly never pass through the lights after amber has changed to red, or anticipate the change to green by moving away on red and amber. The dangers of two 'amber-gamblers' meeting in the middle of a junction are obvious, and you, the motorcyclist, will always come off worse. By all means keep an eye on the lights controlling routes crossing your path so that you have advance warning of when your lights are to change, but do not use this observation to take liberties with the lights. When passing through green lights, always look out for the driver who turns across your bows at the last minute without warning.

Since local authorities do not usually give much warning of filter lights ahead, sooner or later on an unfamiliar road you will probably find yourself coming up to a green left-turn filter when you wish to go straight on. To avoid delaying and irritating drivers behind, pull far enough to the right to allow them safely past on your inside, or even move further over into the space in front of those on the right waiting to go straight ahead over the crossing. If neither of these actions is possible, you should negotiate the turn allowed by the filter and retrace your route when the road conditions allow.

Roundabouts

Positioning and signalling are equally important at roundabouts, and you should strike the right balance between reserve and haste by making a decisive, safe entry into the traffic flow. When traffic is light enough, it should be possible to enter a roundabout where visibility is good only with a reasonable reduction in speed and a change to a lower gear. The experienced rider learns to gauge the speed of traffic coming from the right while he is approaching a roundabout so that he can judge his arrival perfectly in order to merge into the flow without harsh acceleration or braking. Roundabouts are designed to maximise traffic flow by allowing easy entry, but if the traffic is very heavy you will simply have to wait at the entry road for a suitable gap. Do not assume that a vehicle with its left-turn indicator flashing will necessarily turn off before your path of entry.

Priority routes

Priority is sometimes given to a major route passing through a roundabout, so that drivers and motorcyclists already on the roundabout have to give way when they meet this route. Changed priority is made to help in the speeding of traffic flow, but for a rider unfamiliar with the area the need to give way to traffic entering the roundabout can cause a moment's confusion. The advanced rider's obervation skills should always alert him well ahead to an unusual circumstance such as this, but the risk can be reduced by keeping in your correct lane and remembering signalling procedures so that drivers around you are aware of your intentions.

Mini-roundabouts

Mini-roundabouts (especially those where there is a complex of two or three) can cause temporary confusion when you first meet unfamiliar ones, but the extra caution they require is sometimes regarded as their benefit. Since so many people seem unsure of the procedure on them, traffic is slowed down to a safer speed. Local people familiar with the maze may dart around with great confidence, but do not let this delude you into moving faster than is safe for you. Except in the rare instances where road markings indicate differently, treat complexes of mini-roundabouts just like any other roundabout by giving way to traffic coming from your right, and by positioning your bike on the left-hand side of the road if you are in any doubt. Where a mini-roundabout is marked just by white lines on the road, never succumb to the temptation to cut across the island, even if there is no traffic about.

Signalling procedure

On all normal roundabouts you should keep to the established procedure outlined in the *Highway Code* unless lane markings tell you to do differently. If you plan to take the first exit, you should position your bike towards the left kerb and signal a left turn on your approach, keeping the indicator going until you leave the roundabout. If you plan to go more or less straight across, still keep to the left on your approach and through the roundabout, signalling a left turn after you have passed the exit before the one you intend to take. Your anticipation as an advanced rider should have given you plenty of time to move into the left lane on your approach to the

How to tackle a roundabout. Notice that if you intend to take the first exit (centre diagram) or the second (top) then the inside lane is for you, because you will not then have to change lanes while going round. However, the outside lane (bottom) is the right one for you if you are to take the third exit. Always signal your intentions clearly, but not too soon, as you can easily confuse those behind you. However, with signalling, common sense must prevail.

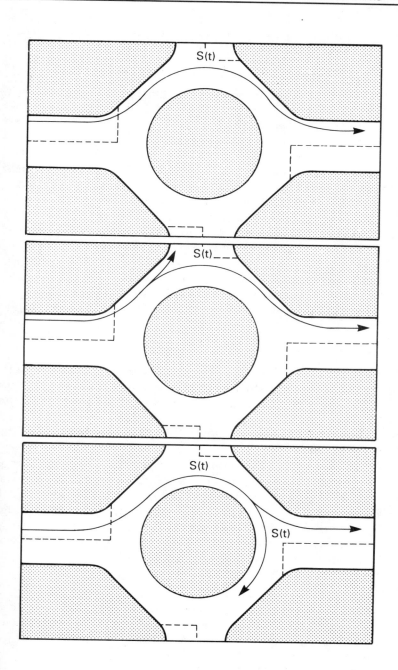

roundabout, but in very heavy traffic you might be obliged to stay over to the right. If this is the case, make sure that other road users are certain of your intentions, and keep firmly to your position. Hold your course until you need to signal left and move over for your exit, glancing over your left shoulder to make sure that you will not be cutting in front of any other vehicles. For exits more than 180 degrees round the roundabout, take the right-hand lane on your approach and signal a right turn before you enter the roundabout. Keep the indicator going until you pass the exit before the one you want, at which point start signalling left and move over for your exit.

Your vulnerability as a motorcyclist in the hurly-burly of traffic flowing through a large and complex roundabout means that considerable commonsense is needed, as well as the usual disciplines of positioning and signalling. Unorthodox roundabouts or gyratory systems with odd shapes and irregularly spaced exits demand that you apply the theories flexibly to fit the circumstances around you.

Summary

- Remember that all junctions create *extra danger*: always signal your intentions well in advance, take up the correct position on the road and move off only when you are certain it is safe to do so; never assume that a vehicle will follow the path suggested by its indicators.
- When *turning right* at a crossroads, pass oncoming vehicles also turning right offside-to-offside, unless road markings or junction layout dictate otherwise.
- Always use the correct positioning and signalling procedure when approaching and negotiating *roundabouts*; your entry to a roundabout should be carefully-judged, decisive and safe.

11

SIGNALS

Giving the correct signals at the right time and in the right way is an essential part of good motorcycling: visible and audible signals are our only means of communication on the road to warn others of our intentions and presence. A rider can also communicate with other road users by his positioning and, with cooperation from them, he can command the situation.

You must bear in mind that signals are used when you are riding in order to inform, not to instruct. Never use signals to give orders to other road users: a signal never gives you the right to make a move, such as a lane change on a dual carriageway or motorway, on the assumption that others will give way. Police officers who deal with accidents are used to hearing the excuse, 'But I gave a signal', from the driver or motorcyclist who has caused the trouble.

The art of proper signalling is a complex part of advanced motorcycling which requires practice as well as learning. As in so many other areas of advanced motorcycling, the ground rules are simple: use only those signals described in the *Highway Code*. Do not make up your own signals or copy those adopted by other people; even if a personal signalling device seems perfectly clear to you, it could be dangerously misleading to someone who sees it for the first time and does not understand what you are trying to 'say'.

You must never expect other road users to react in the right way to your correct signalling. Another driver may not see your signal, or interpret it correctly, or act on it sensibly. Since you can never take it for granted that others will recognise your intentions, always ride so that you can change your plans if your signals are ignored by a careless or thoughtless driver.

Direction indicators

Most of the signals you will make while riding involve your bike's direction indicators, since all new motorcycles have them fitted as standard. A few older models might not have direction indicators; in this case we would recommend fitment of an inexpensive kit of indicators, despite the fact that some purists dislike their appearance.

Direction indicators are used not only for turning left and right, but also for changing your position on the road. Use them thoughtfully and in good time so that other road users know what you are doing and can take action accordingly. The failure to give proper signals is one of the most common faults you see in day-to-day motorcycling – as an advanced rider, make sure that you are never guilty of this. Always use your direction indicators properly at junctions, at roundabouts, when overtaking and when pulling in at the side of the road.

Never think that a signal is unnecessary at quiet times of the day or night just because no-one else seems to be about. At the same time, signals can be used over-zealously: when driving along an urban road dotted with parked cars, there is no need to signal every time you prepare to pass one. In a situation such as this, use your direction indicators intelligently when drivers behind would benefit from knowing about your change of course around a particularly obstructive parked car or a cyclist on a relatively narrow road. Bear in mind also that motorcycle indicators are positioned quite close together, so drivers following at a distance can have difficulty in distinguishing left from right.

The motorcyclist's favourite mistake is forgetting to cancel his indicators after a turn has been made, in spite of a warning light on his bike's instrument panel. If you own a bike equipped with indicators which cancel after a certain time interval, get to know their period so that you are not caught out by them stopping just when you most need them – on a busy roundabout for instance. The advantages of computers to control ignition and fuel injection have been extended to give more sophisticated signal monitoring, and it is even possible to incorporate time, distance and cornering detectors to vary the time before an indicator is automatically cancelled.

Hand signals

The motorcyclist's need for the two basic hand signals – an extended arm to indicate left and right turns – is less now that flashing direction indicators are fitted to all new motorcycles, but there are still occasions when the advanced rider should consider using them (apart from when a bulb or switch fails). A hand signal is advisable when you are not certain that your direction indicator has been seen (in bright sunlight even a normally powerful flashing indicator cannot compete with the sun's rays), or when you need to emphasise your intentions.

A likely instance occurs when you plan to turn off where two side roads are close to each other, and you want to make it clear which one you are going to take. A roundabout with several exits close together provides an opportunity for clarifying your intentions with a hand signal. A right-turn hand signal can be valuable to show that you are intending to turn right and are not just pulling out to pass a parked vehicle. Remember also that these hand signals – as well as the upright palm signal indicating an intention to go straight ahead – can be useful to communicate your plans to a police officer controlling traffic at a junction.

Although you do not often see it used nowadays, the slowing-down signal – an up-and-down movement of the right arm with the palm facing downwards, as if you are repeatedly pressing down on a weight – can also be useful to emphasise the intentions indicated by your brake light. The right time for this signal is when you think that the driver behind is either too close or driving inattentively, and therefore might not realise that you are coming to a halt in traffic. The signal is particularly appropriate when you stop at a pedestrian crossing, since it warns foolish motorists not to overtake as you slow down. At times when taking a hand off the bar might be dangerous, a quick dab on the brakes just to flash the stop light can be used.

There are two hand signals which are now omitted from the *Highway Code*, although some motorcyclists – and car drivers – use them in the belief that they are being courteous to other road users. These are the 'You can overtake me' wave to a following vehicle and the 'Please cross' gesture to pedestrians on a crossing. The problem with these is that if you make a mistake you could be guilty of causing an accident through your good intentions. It is impossible for you to judge, from your position on your bike, whether other road users – drivers or pedestrians – can safely accept your invitation. Leave it to them to make their own judgement. Since irresponsible drivers seem increasingly willing to break the law by overtaking on either side of traffic halted at a pedestrian crossing, the possible consequences of someone stepping into the road at your request do not bear thinking about.

Some modern motorcycles make signalling with the right arm almost impossible to manage because throttle return springs cause the twist grip to wind back when you remove your hand, giving violent deceleration. In the days when hand signals were an essential part of day-to-day motorcycling, bikes were always fitted with some form of friction screw to hold the throttle steady while a right-turn signal was made, but in some markets there is a legal requirement for the throttle to be self-closing. Although there is a school of thought which believes that the hands are better employed on the handlebars than in signalling, we would contend that occasional use of hand signals is a valuable aid to safety, as long as you do not ride one-handed for a moment longer than necessary. If a throttle screw can be fitted, it would be a good idea to have this done. The automatic engine braking effect of a motorcycle when you release the twist grip is appropriate when you make a slowing-down signal, but we would still prefer throttle changes to take place under complete control of the rider's right hand.

The headlight

The IAM recommends that motorcyclists should always ride with the dipped headlight switched on, during the day as well as at night. More than one-third of all accidents involving injury to motorcyclists occur because the other driver has not seen the motorcycle, since bike and rider are relatively inconspicuous on roads dominated by cars, vans and lorries. Keeping the headlight on is compulsory in many countries, and it is highly recommended in Britain. A headlight in front, a red light to the rear and bright clothing in between are a simple means of helping motorcyclists to survive in modern traffic conditions.

While we realise that some experienced riders dislike daytime use of the headlight because they see it as the responsibility of other road users to look out for motorcyclists, our experience proves that a bike is more easily seen when its headlight is illuminated. There are enough car drivers with inadequate concentration or defective vision (as well as short-sighted or careless pedestrians) to confirm the need for motorcyclists to use every aid to visibility at their disposal. There is no point in being theoretically in the right after an accident has occurred.

Keeping the headlight on in daylight also removes the temptation for motorcyclists to imitate those confusing games motorists play with their headlights. Some flash their headlights to say 'Don't move, I'm coming through', while others use exactly the same signal to mean 'Although I'm on the main road I'm slowing down to let you out'. Headlight flashing should be used only in accordance with the instructions laid down by the *Highway Code*, that is as a warning to draw the attention of other road users to your presence.

The brake light

Your brake light cannot be misunderstood by anybody: it works automatically and the message is totally clear. The advanced rider, however, can use his brake light thoughtfully to convey additional information to following drivers. If you consider that a driver is following too closely, it is a good idea when you approach a hazard to brake lightly at first to give him time to drop back to a safe distance before you have to brake more firmly. At times when taking a hand off the handlebar to give a slowing-down signal might be dangerous, an early dab on the brake pedal can give the necessary warning to drivers behind.

Remember to check all your lights – brake light,

indicators, rear light and headlight – frequently since vibration can considerably shorten the life of bulb filaments. It is sensible to carry spare bulbs stowed somewhere on the bike or in the pocket of your regular riding jacket; replacing a failed light quickly could save you from an accident, particularly at night.

Horn

The horn should be sounded when it is necessary to inform other road users of your presence. It should be used sparingly, but you should not be reluctant to use it firmly at the right time as it can be a life-saver. Remember that it is illegal, except in an emergency to avoid an accident, to sound your horn between 11.30pm and 7.00am in a built-up area or at any time of day or night if the bike is stationary. Some motorcyclists feel that safe riding removes the need to use the horn, but there will always be occasions when sounding the horn can be added usefully to all your other safety precautions.

There are three situations when using the horn should be considered. First, it can serve as warning of your approach when the view ahead is very limited, perhaps when nearing a dangerous crossroads where the side roads are obscured by hedges. Second, the horn can be valuable when another road user is vulnerable despite all your safety precautions – cyclists, pedestrians and children might all benefit from a short note on the horn. Third, a firm but polite note on the horn can be used when you are about to overtake another vehicle whose driver may not have noticed you; this consideration is particularly appropriate when passing the driver of a large truck or tractor with limited rearward vision from a noisy cab.

Never use the horn, though, as a substitute for the observation, planning and courtesy which are the mark of a good motorcyclist. Remember that British drivers seem far more ready than their continental counterparts to take offence at the sound of a horn, so use your horn with discretion. If they think that a note on the horn is not delivered politely, some drivers take it as a reprimand, a challenge or an insult, and react accordingly. Thoughtful and courteous use of the horn is what counts. You may not use it often, but to believe that it should never be used is a mistake.

Summary

- Use your *direction indicators* to inform other road users of your intentions, not to give orders to them. Use them correctly, consistently and thoughtfully.
- Use only the *hand signals* given in the *Highway Code*; although direction indicators must always be used, a hand signal should be given in circumstances where other road users would benefit from emphasis of your intentions.
- Ride with your *dipped headlight* illuminated at all times, day and night: this practice helps to reduce the chances of other road users failing to see you.
- Use the *horn* when it would be valuable to give other road users added warning of your approach.

12

ROAD-CRAFT IN TOWN AND COUNTRY

Although the systematic riding method outlined in Chapter 3 equips you to deal with all kinds of roads and hazards, there are differences between riding conditions in town and country which call for special knowledge and the use of different techniques by the advanced motorcyclist. Little pieces of local knowledge, the wisdom gained from experience of different conditions and the almost instinctive ability to predict what other road users will do add up to 'road-craft'; this may be an abstract concept, but it is one which separates the advanced motorcyclist from other riders.

Riding in town

A large proportion of motorcycling is done in built-up areas since so many people ride to and from work, and the special difficulties of urban conditions are increasing as traffic becomes more and more congested. Riding in town demands sustained concentration and an even higher degree of observation than in rural conditions. Traffic is heavier, situations change more quickly, buildings and vehicles restrict views, and the frequency of road junctions provides many more accident possibilities.

Local knowledge is invaluable in town, athough you must always guard against dropping your level of concentration simply because you are riding in familiar territory. Whenever the advanced motorcyclist ventures on to new routes, however, he consciously records their features in order to remember important junctions, badly congested areas, one-way systems, roundabouts and filter lights; the more he can commit to memory, the more familiar the route will be next time. Whether or not you are riding over known roads, keep trying to observe what is happening to the traffic flow ahead by positioning yourself carefully to maximise your view past the vehicles in front. Watch for the pattern of junctions coming up and get in the correct line of traffic well in advance. If you find yourself stuck in the wrong lane and cannot safely move to the right one, you must keep to your committed path and use your sense of direction to find another route back to the right road.

Route observation

Shrewd observation can often provide you with valuable snippets of information which a less skilled rider would miss. Keeping an eye on large lorries or buses well down a line of traffic can give you early warning of a halt. Look ahead for bus-stop signs and note passengers crowding towards the doors of a bus ready to get off. Always be prepared for taxis to move off, stop suddenly or make a U-turn, especially if the 'hire' sign is lit and the cab might be hailed; shopping streets and railway stations are places where you need to be particularly vigilant for unexpected actions by taxi drivers. Lines of parked cars present potential hazards for motorcyclists: treat a car with special care if you can see an occupant who may throw open the door in your path, and watch for the tell-tale signs – a driver at the wheel, a puff of smoke from the exhaust, reversing lights lit or front wheels angling out – which reveal that a car is about to pull out.

Pedestrians

Pedestrians are another potential hazard to the motorcyclist. Lines of parked cars or a row of stationary traffic are places where a pedestrian may pop through a gap without expecting a motorcyclist to be coming. The advanced rider will be particularly careful where shoppers might step off a crowded pavement, or near particular buildings – schools, factories, railway stations or pubs – where crowds of people may be present at certain times of day. Special care is needed where pedestrians cross at traffic lights: people can quite easily step into the road without glancing to see whether it is clear, and if a large number of pedestrians is streaming across in front of you it is quite possible that a few tail-enders following the flock will cross as your lights are changing to green. The motorcyclist must be alert for pedestrians making sudden movements across the road, perhaps to take advantage of a gap in the traffic without looking carefully enough to notice your presence. Watch for small movements – a turn of the head, a wave or a brisk walk towards the kerb – which may indicate a pedestrian's next move.

Pedal cyclists

Give pedal cyclists a wide berth, as they may lack your road sense and make sudden movements. Beware of the cyclist who emerges from a side street without looking, and never forget that any cyclist is entitled to his wobble, as a High Court ruling has confirmed. It is the motorcyclist's responsibility to avoid a cyclist.

Passing the queue

When traffic is very heavy, the motorcyclist can often take advantage of room to thread his way past lines of slow-moving or stationary cars and lorries, but such opportunities should be taken only when gaps are wide enough to be negotiated without danger. Watch very carefully for pedestrians who will not be expecting you, and for the few bad-tempered drivers who show their resentment of the motorcyclist's greater freedom by deliberately trying to block your path. Fall back into line when in doubt, and wait patiently for safe overtaking opportunities to present themselves again.

Lane discipline

Lane discipline is vital in the one-way systems used in many larger towns to keep heavy volumes of traffic moving. Motorcyclists have to be especially careful to look ahead and notice turns out of the system in time to take up position among a stream of nose-to-tail cars in the appropriate lane. Keep to the left, unless this lane leads to a mandatory left turn you do not want to follow or you plan to turn right. Overtaking is permissible on both sides on one-way streets, but if you pass vehicles on the nearside be alert to the possibility of some of them suddenly moving into your path in order to turn left. Watch out for pedestrian crossings in one-way streets, as these can often be almost completely obscured by congested traffic.

Road surfaces

Urban road surfaces are usually more slippery than country roads because the coating of oil and rubber on city streets tends to become polished by constant traffic. Special care is needed even in dry weather, but after a shower urban roads can become treacherous. Oil also accumulates on the road at any places where vehicles stop regularly, such as at traffic lights, so allow for the possibility of greatly reduced tyre grip when braking and accelerating.

Traffic lights

When you stop at traffic lights, you should always select neutral and release the clutch lever while waiting for the lights to change. This avoids unnecessary wear to the clutch and removes the danger of the sudden jerk forward which would occur if your left hand slipped off the clutch lever while you were in gear. For the same reasons, holding your bike stationary on a hill by slipping the clutch is bad practice. If you have stopped on a hill, always allow a little extra room in case the vehicle in front should roll back. The driver may not have applied the handbrake firmly enough, or may make such a clumsy start that his vehicle rolls back a couple of feet before it moves forward.

Confidence in queues

Before we leave the subject of riding in town, it is worth observing that motorcyclists and drivers who are used to the very dense, sometimes swift-moving traffic of large cities are generally more confident. London riders and drivers, in particular, have a decisive style which seems almost foolhardy to people from quieter parts of the country, but by and large it works well because they know what they are doing and where they are going. The 'press-on' approach helps to move large volumes of traffic through some very congested road systems.

There can be no more vivid illustration of this style than the behaviour of dispatch riders in large cities. Before dismissing the whole breed as lunatics, it is worth considering that anyone earning a living on a bike has to stay in one piece. Some of their manoeuvres would produce an immediate failure under IAM test conditions, but the skill of the top-class dispatch riders cannot be denied, especially when one realises that 30,000 to 50,000 miles a year is unexceptional to them. The use of this skill to negotiate metropolitan traffic congestion cannot be condoned, but it can perhaps be tolerated by the advanced rider.

Conversely, applying a decisive style to gaps in the traffic when riding on a provincial town's roads can seem aggressive, even downright dangerous, partly because it is out of place. In the same way, someone riding warily in London for the first time must try not to be intimidated by the cut-and-thrust of somewhere like Hyde Park Corner in the rush hour. Each type of progress is right for the conditions, so it can be dangerous if you do not – or even feel that you cannot – conform to the traffic pattern around you. The advice can really only be this: 'When in Rome, do as the Romans do'.

Riding in the country

Although the basic rules of motorcycling remain the same in all environments, riding on open roads needs a completely different set of road-craft abilities. Country roads with little traffic give the motorcyclist a chance to exercise his riding abilities to the full, and to enjoy the pleasure of taking varying bends with a rhythm which can never be built up in town.

Route observation

Your need to assess the road ahead is just as important in the country as in town, but the signs to look for (apart from the normal ones erected by local authorities) can vary. The list is almost endless, but one hallmark of the advanced rider is that he can recognise information useful to him. A few examples can illustrate the point so that you get used to practising selective and shrewd observation.

Canals and railways, even though disused, may mean hump-back bridges are not far away. A line of telegraph poles ahead can indicate the severity of a hidden bend, although do not rely on this since telegraph poles can track straight on when a road bends. Any livestock in the fields would suggest that you should watch for mud and slime on the road near any gateways or farms. The lie of trees and hedges can indicate the steepness of any incline. A few isolated houses are points where you need to take extra care in case people or domestic animals appear.

Full advantage should be taken of the views often available across open spaces of stretches of road in the distance. You can give yourself early warning of a wide lorry approaching on a narrow road if you see it through a gap in the trees, or of a car on a converging side-road if you notice it briefly through a gateway. Any special features you remember about the road could be useful to you on another journey over the same route, so take note of bad patches of surface, deceptive bends and temporary obstacles.

Road surfaces

Country road surfaces, particularly on smaller roads, can throw many surprises at the unwary motorcyclist. The combination of a series of bends between high walls or hedges can conceal all manner of dangers, such as potholes, mud, patches of ice, deep puddles, streams of water across the road, tightening-radius bends, dead animals, wet leaves and a strange variety of cambers and bumps. The relative lack of traffic on such roads often tempts even experienced riders into travelling too fast for safety, so always make very sure that you ride at a speed which allows you to stop within the distance you can see. Expect a tractor or a herd of cows around every blind bend.

Rural roads

Just as important, you should always be careful to maintain a safe stopping distance when following other vehicles along country roads. Some motorcyclists are prone to pressing too close, particularly if they generally ride in urban areas where speeds are much lower and safe braking distances shorter. Keep a proper braking distance even if you are overtaken, and do not fall into the trap of allowing an inadequate distance just because you can see round or over the car in front; just occasionally, perhaps if another car emerges suddenly from a side road, the car in front will stop more quickly than you expect. Since so few car drivers leave a safe distance, do not take the gap left by others as some sort of standard for yourself.

Technique

The experienced motorcyclist shows good lane discipline on dual carriageways with two or three lanes. He uses the nearside lane unless he wishes to overtake, although when traffic is busy he may spend much of his time in the centre or outside lanes. It is worth remembering that while such roads often allow the same 70mph speed limit as motorways, you are quite likely to encounter an added range of hazards, such as side turnings to the left without slip roads, traffic slowing down in the outside lane in order to turn right, and slow-moving vehicles such as tractors or milk-floats. It is not worth seeking the fastest convoys by moving from one lane to another on a busy road: each lane change is an unnecessary danger and frequently offers no advantage.

Obey the white line markings implicitly on ordinary two-way roads. All are put there for your safety, especially the continuous lines which prevent overtaking. If the road is wide enough, you can often overtake a slower car without crossing a continuous centre line; but never do this on a blind bend, and only embark on such a manoeuvre if you are certain that the driver ahead knows that you are coming through and will not squeeze you over the central lines into the path of oncoming traffic. Be very careful on two-way roads with a third lane in the centre available to overtaking vehicles moving in either direction. Since these roads can be perilous at the best of times, the motorcyclist, who is not as conspicuous as a car, should overtake only when there is no chance of an inattentive oncoming car driver moving into this lane at the same time.

Smooth overtaking leaves plenty of clearance between a car and a motorcycle, yet keeps the rider well within the double white lines. The rider will ensure that he has accelerated well clear of the car before starting his move back to his normal position on the road.

Knowing your route

You will enjoy any journey over major or minor country roads, and travel in greater safety, if you have prepared your route in advance. All your concentration is available for safe riding if you do not have to search for signposts, worry about getting lost and make frequent stops to check a map. It is a very good idea to memorise your route before you leave home, or make notes of landmark towns, villages and junctions on a piece of card which can be stuck to the top of your fuel tank.

Experience

As we leave the subject of riding in town and country, it should be emphasised that the road-craft which all advanced motorcyclists acquire comes only from experienced and practised observation. So much skill and knowledge is required that a motorcyclist continues to refine his abilities throughout his riding career – to cover the intricacies of every possible situation is beyond the scope of any book. This chapter is intended to show the type of problems encountered, to give the reader some basic clues to help in improving his abilities for himself, and to encourage him to meet the high standards of road-craft needed for the IAM's test.

Summary

- *Road-craft* is a complicated but essential skill which is the hallmark of the advanced motorcyclist. Absorb all the guidance – important little details of *observation and technique* – contained in this chapter so that you can develop your road-craft.
- Understand the differences in applying road-craft on *town and country* roads.

13

MOTORWAYS

Motorways sometimes have their attractions for the motorcyclist. After the congestion which goes with riding in towns or on busy trunk roads, the escape on to an open stretch of motorway can raise a rider's spirits as he winds up the engine to a comfortable cruising speed, looks forward to making fast progress with no intersections, runs on a good surface and rides with a good view of the road ahead. A couple of hours later, however, he may feel differently, yearning for some 'real riding' on an old-fashioned trunk road. The continuous vibration of high-speed riding, the stiffness of body and limbs which hardly change position, constant speed and unchanging noise add up to a feeling of fatigue and numbness of the mind which remind him that motorcycling on motorways is not much fun.

Some of the rigours of motorway riding are reduced if you have a large-capacity bike designed for touring, but even on a comfortable, high-geared machine long stints on a motorway can be monotonous. It is important, therefore, to ask yourself whether you really want to ride on motorways and, if so, for how long?

Taking in a stretch of motorway can make a short trip quicker and more relaxed, but if you plan to make a longer journey which involves riding for most of the day it is worth trying to follow a route which mixes trunk roads and motorways. Many motorways run reasonably parallel to the trunk roads they were designed to supersede, so you can generally plot a route which uses a combination of both. A good plan is to use motorways to pass large towns and cities, but take to trunk roads for the sake of variety where these might offer some appealing ordinary road riding. If you cannot avoid spending most of a long journey on the motorway, build in enough time to allow for regular stops at service stations to stretch your limbs and rest your mind.

Terminology

Before dealing with the techniques of advanced riding on motorways, some brief words are necessary about terminology. Some people describe the three lanes of a motorway as the 'slow', 'middle' and 'fast' lanes: this is misleading, since speed alone does not determine the use of lanes, and to describe a lane as 'fast' smacks of irresponsibility. More usual practice is to use the terms 'inside', 'centre' and 'outside', but as more and more motorway sections with four lanes are being constructed this nomenclature is becoming outdated and could be confusing. The best way is the notation used by the police, and this is what we shall follow in this chapter. Each lane is simply given a number: therefore, lane 1 is the 'inside', lane 2 the 'centre' and lane 3 the 'outside', with lane 4 used where applicable.

Joining a motorway

The motorway slip road should be used to accelerate to a speed which matches that of the traffic in lane 1. Signal a right turn so that anyone in lane 1 will notice you, and maybe move over to lane 2 to give you plenty of room. Your run along the stretch of the slip road adjoining the main carriageway should be timed so that you can slip neatly into place as soon as possible without losing speed, but keep a wary eye on the timid driver who may be slowing down at the end of the slip road to wait for a larger gap in the traffic. In extreme cases, this kind of driver – who is as much of a menace to himself as to other road users – may even stop at the end of the slip road as if to give way.

You should remain in lane 1 for at least half a mile to adjust yourself to the speed and assess the traffic pattern behind you. As a motorcyclist, your cruising speed will probably mean that you will spend a good proportion of your motorway journey in lane 2, so move over (after the usual mirror check and right turn signal) when it becomes necessary. Return to lane 1 whenever it is reasonably clear after overtaking manoeuvres have been completed. Lane 3 is *not* the fast lane which many people take it to be, so use it only for overtaking.

Motorway discipline

Your speed should be a steady pace at which you and your bike feel comfortable, and one which is appropriate to weather conditions and traffic density – but it must not be over 70mph. You should not treat 70mph as an obligatory speed: it is a limit, not a target. Travelling a few miles per hour under the limit will make little difference to your journey time, and may be more relaxing if you have a long stretch on the motorway ahead of you. Just because some people choose to put their licences at risk – and endanger everybody by creating greater speed differentials – by breaking the limit does not mean that you should copy them to demonstrate the potency of your machine.

Lane discipline

Once you have settled into a steady cruising speed, glance in the mirrors frequently so that you are constantly aware of all the vehicles around you. Maintain strict lane discipline, so that you are always in the appropriate lane for your speed and the traffic conditions. Poor lane discipline, generally from car drivers, is one of the most common examples of thoughtless behaviour on motorways, and it can occasionally play its part in an accident when it forces drivers or riders into lane 3. Far too often on motorways you see more traffic travelling in lane 3 than lanes 1 and 2. For your own safety, ride in the centre of your lane so that motorists are not tempted to pass you in the same lane with inches to spare.

If you come up behind a 'lane hog' who fails to move over when there is plenty of space available, do not resort to aggressive tactics. Remember that the principles of good motorcycling require you to maintain a proper braking distance, so be patient and wait for an opportunity to overtake safely. Never overtake on the inside: as well as being a serious offence, this can be dangerous because no motorist expects it to happen. If a driver knocked you off as you tried it, the blame for the accident would be laid squarely at your door – if you were still alive to worry about it.

Keep your distance

Keeping a safe distance between your motorcycle and the vehicle in front is even more important than good lane discipline. The importance of leaving room for seeing, reacting and braking has already been explained elsewhere in this book, but maintaining a safe distance is particularly relevant on a motorway. As the sensation of speed inevitably becomes dulled, it is all too easy to close up on the vehicle ahead so that the distance between you is nothing like adequate in an emergency; keep reminding yourself of this point, by checking the speedometer if it helps to bring home to you the speeds being ridden.

You are deluding yourself if you think that riding within this safe distance is acceptable because you can see several vehicles ahead. This foolish attitude ignores all kinds of possibilities: the driver ahead might brake suddenly if he sees a piece of debris in the road, a vehicle from the opposing carriageway might crash through the central reservation, or the vehicle ahead might even suffer a tyre blow-out. Another reason why people fail to leave a safe gap is that overtaking vehicles often slot into the space you have allowed; all you can do is throttle back for a moment and drop back accordingly.

Overtaking

Overtaking must be carried out strictly according to the systematic method of control: rear observation, signal, gearchange if necessary, rear observation and pull out to pass, accelerating if appropriate. The higher speeds of motorways mean that adhering meticulously to the basic safety points is vital during overtaking. You should have your headlight on as a visual reminder of your presence for motorists who might not take you in when looking for cars in their rear-view mirrors. When passing a line of slower vehicles, it is a good idea to leave your right turn indicator flashing as a further reminder until you are about to return to lane 1 or 2. Many riders and drivers signal a left turn at the end of the manoeuvre, but this is really quite unnecessary in normal circumstances.

Changing lanes

When planning a lane change, take special care with your rear observation. Judging speeds in the mirror is very difficult, and sudden acceleration by drivers behind will not be noticeable until the last moment. Assume that any car coming up in your mirror is moving fast, and delay any planned overtaking of your own until it has gone by. For the sake of your own safety, allow cars pressing too close behind to pass by.

Slip road courtesy

As you approach and pass an entrance slip road, it is necessary to keep an eye on any traffic which may be about to join the motorway. If it is quite safe for you to move from lane 1 to lane 2 without worrying a driver coming up behind, it is courteous to do so in order to make life easier for the driver joining the motorway, as well as removing the chance of an accident caused by this driver failing to spot you. This forethought will be especially appreciated by lorry drivers, who are less able to adjust their speed to blend into the traffic flow. If a slip road is very busy, this tactic is particularly appropriate.

Abnormal motorway conditions

A multiple pile-up on a fogbound motorway occurs almost every winter because so many drivers travel too fast and too close together for the conditions. The poor motorcyclist has little chance of escaping serious injury or death in these catastrophic accidents, so as long as so much bad driving persists the only worthwhile advice must be to avoid motorways in fog; indeed it is best if you can avoid riding in fog altogether.

Motorway fog

If you do find fog coming down while riding on a motorway, your actions should be governed by just the same rules which apply to coping with fog on other roads (see Chapter 17 for detailed advice). Keep down to a speed which gives safe braking distance within your range of vision, try to keep to lane 1 or 2, and ensure that you are riding with your dipped headlight on.

Motorway warning signals

Automatic motorway signals give you a recommended maximum speed during fog, on the approach to an incident or even during heavy rain, as well as giving warning of lane closures ahead or even the need to stop or leave the motorway in the event of a serious accident. Many people do not understand these signals, so it is worth studying the range of warnings shown in the accompanying diagram. Some drivers and riders, furthermore, do not respect these signals, believing that they have been left on by mistake if no obvious need for them can be seen. It is worth confirming, therefore, that the police are extremely diligent in employing these signals when they are necessary and in switching them off again as soon as a danger is cleared. Always obey them, because they serve as warning that a hazard does exist, perhaps a mile or two down the carriageway.

These warning signals are so often abused that you may see in your mirror a car closing quite quickly. Since it is very difficult to judge the speed of a vehicle approaching from behind, it pays to exercise extreme caution and delay any planned lane-change of your own until the vehicle in question is well out of the way. If the signals show that you will need to make a lane-change, perhaps because an accident has blocked one or two lanes, make your manoeuvre in good time and keep below the speed indicated. Keep a careful eye open for the fast-approaching driver in an empty lane who dives into the slowing traffic stream at the last minute.

Crosswinds

Since speeds are normally higher on motorways you need to be alert to the increased effect of crosswinds, which can

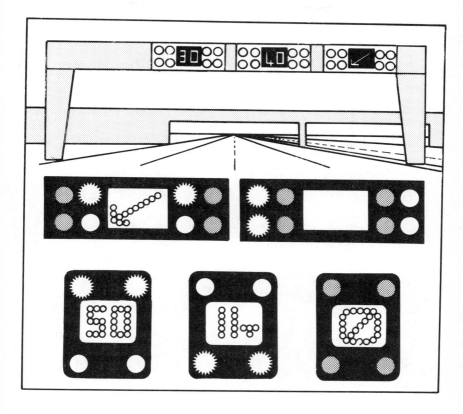

Some motorway signs. The upper part of this diagram illustrates the gantry which displays the signs, which in this case are showing speed restrictions and an imminent lane closure on a three-lane carriageway. The central part of the drawing shows how the various restrictions are accompanied by flashing lights. The lower part shows other signs that you may come across on the motorway, displaying (l–r) temporary speed limit, lane 3 closed ahead and the 'clearway' sign, which is not accompanied by flashing lights, to show that the temporary restrictions have finished.

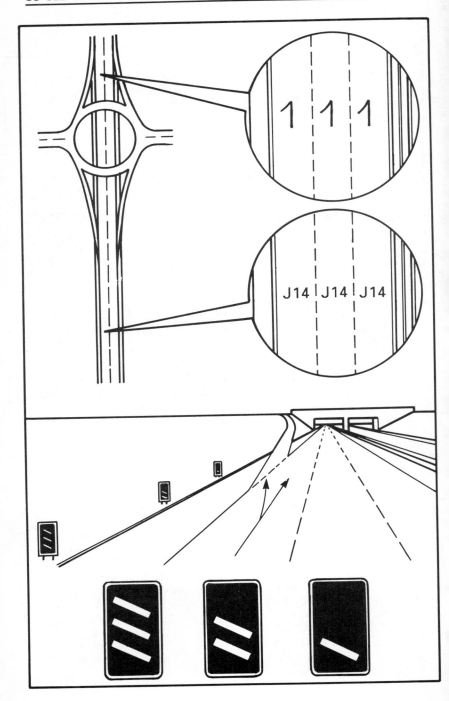

push your bike off course. You may feel this wherever a motorway passes across open country or through a cutting. Dropping as low on the tank as your back and hand controls will allow is your obvious response, particularly for head winds, and the rider soon learns to lean instinctively into a side wind to compensate for the pressure. He must be prepared constantly for the sharply changing wind pressures caused by bridges, cuttings and passing other vehicles. Coaches and large lorries work up to much higher speeds on motorways, so be ready for severe turbulence – which can throw you right off course – when passing or being passed by one of these vehicles. The effect of the wind will also vary as the motorway changes direction, but this is gradual enough to be easily allowed for.

Leaving the motorway

Taking an exit from a motorway involves a very simple procedure. Generally junction signs are posted 1-mile and ½-mile in advance, followed by three-, two- and one-bar signs which provide a countdown starting at 300 yards. It is obvious that you must synchronise your speed with the traffic in lane 1, making sure that you have completed your manoeuvre into this lane well before the three-bar sign appears; in very heavy traffic, you should slot into lane 1 (after checking your mirror and signalling a left turn) even earlier than this – soon after the 1-mile sign if necessary. If you are already travelling in lane 1, signal a left turn in good time and certainly before you pass the three-bar sign.

Entering the slip road is a potentially hazardous moment. After riding for maybe a couple of hours at close to the legal limit, your judgement of speed will have

Carriageway markings on a motorway include a warning that a junction is near (J14 in this case) and, once the junction is passed, a half-chevron indicating that traffic is merging from the left. The distance markers (below) are not restricted to motorways, and indicate the distance, in hundreds of yards, to the next point at which a rider may leave a motorway or other route, or a roundabout.

become distorted. Since 50mph will seem more like 30mph, it is very easy to approach the roundabout too quickly and end up having to brake heavily. Some slip roads curve so sharply that the dangers of misjudging your braking become even greater. Rely on your bike's speedometer when making this big speed adjustment; glancing down at the road surface flashing by close to your feet can also ram home the point.

It is worth pointing out that it is possible to become 'speed happy' while you are still on the motorway. We have already mentioned the tendency for your judgement of braking distance to lapse, but you should also remember that a violent swerve – perhaps just to avoid metal, rubber or rope on the road – could cause you to fall off your machine, simply because you attempt a manoeuvre which you would never normally contemplate at such high speed.

While on the subject of speed, a few words are also necessary about the dangers of unaccustomed speeds. Some riders deliberately take a bike – maybe a new machine much more powerful than its predecessor, or a borrowed one – on to the motorway to find out how fast it will go. While deserted motorways are definitely the safest place to become familiar with how a bike feels at high speed, the rider must take care to increase speed gradually rather than blast straight up to the 70mph range. You need time to get the feel of a new bike – the response of the controls and differences in layout – before riding fast, and cautious use in traffic is vital to avoid the danger of sudden braking leading to a skid on an unfamiliar machine.

Keeping your motorcycle in trim

To give their best at prolonged high speeds, tyres sometimes need to be inflated a few pounds per square inch harder than normal. Our speed limits and the frequency with which riders hop on and off motorways mean that this precaution is more appropriate to riding on the continent, but the higher speeds of motorways do mean that checking the pressure and condition of your tyres becomes even more important. Analyses of motorway accidents have shown that one in six is caused by tyre failure, so pay good attention to your tyres to minimise the chance of this dreadful possibility happening to you.

Motorway breakdowns are often caused by factors which a diligent rider can avoid. Do not push your bike beyond its limitations in age or design, and ensure that it is in the best possible condition to cope with the vibration of continuous high speed and the unusual stresses on engine, transmission and frame. Make sure that oil level is near the maximum, as consumption often increases at high speed. Think carefully about fuel level to avoid running out between service areas, as most petrol tanks give a range of little more than 120 miles – about two hours' riding on the motorway.

If you are ever forced to stop on a motorway, pull over to the far left of the hard shoulder (use of the hard shoulder, of course, is permissible only in an emergency). Leave your rear light and indicators on as warning to other drivers, and either stay with your bike to wait for a police patrol vehicle or start walking to the nearest emergency telephone. Red arrows on the marker posts (at 100 metre intervals) indicate the direction of the nearest one, which will never be more than half a mile away; be sure to walk on the hard shoulder and not the motorway itself. If you are able to resume your journey, do not pull straight on to the main carriageway after moving off; treat the hard shoulder as an acceleration lane, making your move to lane 1 only when your speed matches that of the vehicles around you.

Summary

- Ask yourself whether you really *need* to ride on a motorway: using ordinary trunk roads for sections of a long journey can be preferable to the monotony of motorway riding.
- When *joining* a motorway, accelerate up the slip road to a speed which matches that of the traffic in lane 1 and move into this lane when it is safe to do so.
- Treat the 70mph speed limit *as a limit*, not a target which you must reach.

- Remember the two essential disciplines of motorway riding: maintain a *safe braking distance* at all times and watch your *lane discipline*.
- Be alert to the dangers of *fog* and *crosswinds*; your bike can be pushed off course by strong winds, or even by the turbulence from lorries and coaches.
- Motorway *warning signals* are always illuminated for a reason: obey them at all times.
- When planning to *leave* a motorway, ensure that you have slotted into lane 1 well before the three-bar sign.

14

ECONOMICAL RIDING

The fact that motorcycling is so much cheaper than motoring is part of its appeal for riders of lightweight machines and step-throughs, but there is also scope for the superbike owner to benefit from advanced riding. While road conditions, traffic and the type of motorcycle you own all affect how far you manage to travel on each gallon of fuel, the basic principles of advanced motorcycling tend to go hand in hand with economical riding. Anticipating hazards well in advance, braking in good time, and using the throttle smoothly and progressively all contribute to fuel economy, better tyre wear and less frequent brake pad replacement.

The motorcycle you buy

The type of motorcycle you buy will influence fuel consumption just as much as the way you ride it, so there is no point in buying a more powerful or larger motorcycle than you need. Using all the acceleration of a superbike can result in staggeringly high fuel consumption, so you need to find a compromise between the level of performance you want and how much you are prepared to pay for it. Choosing a motorcycle is really a case of horses for courses. A small two-stroke designed for economical commuting will use lots of fuel, wear out quickly and be tiring to ride if it is used for screaming along 20 miles of dual-carriageway every day. Equally, a large, low-revving touring bike will be inappropriate if most of your riding is in tight city streets.

You will need to comb through the motorcycle magazines to obtain an idea about the fuel consumption merits of particular makes and models. Road tests usually state the fuel consumption achieved, but bear in mind that this may reflect a great deal of hard riding to obtain performance figures; magazine figures will invariably be lower than you will achieve, but they can be useful in comparing one bike with another. It pays to note that fuel consumption is not always proportional to capacity: a high-performance two-stroke machine of 500cc might do about 32mpg while a bigger four-stroke touring bike of 1000cc might return 43mpg. Large variations can occur between machines of similar capacity and style: one 124cc four-stroke commuting bike manages 103 mpg while another does only 85mpg.

The type of petrol used has always been an important factor for car owners, but concern about lead pollution has brought a new interest in the subject. While an increasing number of car owners have converted their engines to unleaded petrol, and most new models are so designed from scratch, the modern motorcyclist can feel superior and more environmentally clean because most Japanese engines, from their introduction, have accepted two-star and/or unleaded varieties of fuel. The new-generation multi-cylinder BMWs will also accept unleaded fuel, along with the more recent flat-twins. For older motorcycles, some of the Italian exotica and similar high performance mounts, it is essential to check the manufacturer's recommendations before considering a change to unleaded riding.

Once you have a shortlist of choices, it is worth checking the price of essential spares – items such as oil filter elements, chains, plugs, points and bulbs – as there can be surprising differences between makes. Find out what the service charges are likely to be if you do not intend to carry out your own maintenance. Although it is beyond the scope of this book, depreciation is the other major factor to consider when working out costs; a glance through the second-hand bikes listed in the classified advertisements in a weekly motorcycling paper can give you an idea of how your chosen make and model is likely to compare with others.

Techniques for economy

Having chosen your machine, you need to ride in the manner which will obtain the best from it, remembering that the techniques of advanced motorcycling generally help to achieve good fuel consumption. Regardless of your bike, the best aid to economy is your right hand, since taking care to accelerate progressively, to slow down in good time and to feather back the throttle when cruising all produce savings of as much as 10 per cent, depending upon your style of riding. If you can manage to increase your average by 5mpg, you will save around £40 in a typical 10,000 mile year.

If you want to test just how well you can do, try running for a tankful with a self-imposed rev limit well below the engine's normal maximum, and see how much further you can travel before refuelling. If you start with the tank full to the brim and then brim it again when you need to refuel, you can work out an exact consumption figure. Tearing up to the red line in every gear makes little difference to journey times; as well as increasing fuel consumption it also wears out your bike's engine, chains and tyres more quickly.

Riding for economy, however, although it is to be encouraged, must never be allowed to come before considerations of safety. It is quite conceivable that a motorcyclist can find himself in a potentially dangerous situation, perhaps through being unwilling to accelerate briskly when it is necessary, simply because he has allowed petrol saving to become more important than planned, systematic and constructive advanced riding. Staying in a high gear for too long can be dangerous when road and traffic conditions call for a change down to be in the right gear at the right time, and causing the engine to labour increases the stresses on it.

A few other warnings need to be made about excessive zeal in riding for economy. You should never coast down hills or when coming to a halt, for reasons already explained in Chapter 8. Do not ride so slowly that you become a danger to other road users and to yourself. Do not over-inflate the tyres to save petrol, as the manufacturer's recommended pressures give the best roadholding, braking and wear rates. Take care not to push in the choke (if your bike has one) too early after a cold start, as you could stall in the middle of your first junction.

It is important to keep your bike running in the best state of tune. Maladjusted ignition and carburettors, as well as worn spark plugs, can affect fuel economy adversely. Routine service attention should also include checks on brakes and wheel alignment; any problems here can add to the resistance which your bike's engine must overcome to propel it. Fuel savings can also be made by planning your route to avoid congested areas as far as possible: steady cruising in top gear along the motorway can use less fuel than stop-start progress on a shorter route.

Summary

- Think about economy when you *choose your motorcycle*. How much performance do you need? What size engine? Two-stroke or four-stroke?
- While the principles of *advanced motorcycling* generally help fuel economy, think about how you can use the advice in this chapter to improve economy still further; but avoid putting economy before safety or riding so slowly that you are a nuisance to other road users.

15

NIGHT RIDING

Night riding is an essential part of motorcycling, but for many inexperienced riders the occasion when they first venture out in darkness, or away from the reassuring glow of street lights, is a worrying one. Like all other aspects of handling a motorcycle safely, however, night riding presents no undue risks as long as you observe the rules. Indeed, there are positive advantages to riding at night, when traffic begins to thin out – the experience can be less stressful and your journey time can be reduced. But riding in the dark can be dangerous if you do not obey the rules, especially on a long run when you are feeling tired. Always remember the extra dangers of allowing your concentration to lapse, because accident rates per vehicle mile do rise dramatically at night.

Lighting equipment

Your motorcycle should be examined frequently to ensure safety: your lights should all be clean and work properly, and the headlight should be correctly adjusted. On older bikes, the headlight can be adjusted quite easily by loosening the screws on each side and swivelling the unit until the right beam height is obtained. The level can be set by shining the light at a wall and setting the beam at the height recommended in the manufacturer's handbook, or by taking the bike out for a short trial run before your journey starts. Remember to alter the level to compensate for the weight of a pillion passenger or heavy luggage, and have the headlight set up in advance if your journey will start in daylight and end in darkness.

Although most motorcycles are now equipped with a powerful quartz-halogen headlight which throws a reasonably long and intense beam, those fitted with old-fashioned tungsten filaments can give you an inadequate view at night. If you are unhappy about the lighting of tungsten bulbs on your machine, it would be well worth asking your dealer about a quartz-halogen conversion. As long as the bike's alternator or generator has the capacity to cope with the bigger power demand, it should be possible to fit a complete light assembly into the headlight shell. Alternatively, you could consider buying one of the numerous spotlights or foglights available from accessory shops.

There is one aspect of motorcycle design – rear lighting – which falls far behind accepted standards for cars. At the time of writing, only a few makes of motorcycle incorporate high-intensity rear foglights; worse still, there are few rear mudguards or tail fairings which will easily accept an auxiliary light unit. Even so, if much winter or night riding is contemplated, every effort should be made to fit a suitable lamp. The types sold for trailers or caravans, often described as 'bulkhead fitting', are usually the easiest to adapt.

A motorcycle's vibration makes all light bulbs prone to failure at any time, and you have a more serious problem than a car driver if the headlight or rear light fails at night. Carry spare bulbs with you all the time, making sure that you wrap them well (if you carry them in a pocket) so that fragments of broken glass cannot cut you if you crash. Check the rear light and brake light from time to time during a long journey, and look over the condition of wiring, snap connectors and terminals before setting out on a night ride. Wiring might fray or a connector separate, particularly on an older machine, raising the frightening possibility of a sudden black-out.

Eyesight and fatigue

It is just as important to make sure that the rider, as well as his machine, is properly prepared for night riding. Since any sight deficiencies are relatively worse at night, make sure your eyes are tested regularly by an optician. Should you be in any doubt about your vision being worse in darkness than during the day, have your eyes tested for night riding purposes; an optician will be able to prescribe spectacles accordingly if you need them. It is vital that your visor or goggles are in good condition and clean, since any speck of dirt, smear of grease or scratch will distort and reflect light, making the already taxing task of night observation even harder.

Travelling any distance after dark is undoubtedly more exhausting than daylight riding, with fatigue making itself felt first as eye strain caused by looking along the headlight beam, avoiding being dazzled by the lights of other vehicles and keeping your powers of observation razor-sharp. You can help to reduce the risk of tiredness by trying to avoid making a long journey at night after a strenuous day. A snack before starting is better than a heavy meal, which might make you feel drowsy. Certainly keep off all alcohol, as your judgement and concentration deteriorate after just one drink. Never take pills to stay awake, since such drugs can have dangerous side-effects which affect your ability on the road. Heavier clothing will be needed to keep you warm in lower night-time temperatures, not just for comfort but also to keep your circulation and reaction times normal.

Keep asking yourself throughout your journey whether you feel at all tired, and stop for a break if you do. Stretch your arms and legs, and rest your eyes; you could even go for a short but vigorous run up the road to get your circulation going again. Some experienced riders carry a flask of hot coffee or tea to help to restore their senses when a break is necessary. The monotony of motorways at night can lead to a particularly dangerous state of fatigue and poor concentration, so plan to make regular stops at service areas (never on the hard shoulder). Changing your cruising speed from time to time to vary the engine note, vibration and wind pressure can also help you to stay alert on a motorway.

Dazzle and visibility

Novices invariably find that their biggest worry about riding at night is glare from the headlights of oncoming vehicles. Most people find that at first their eyes are drawn involuntarily towards approaching headlights, but in time they learn to make a conscious effort to look away and concentrate the gaze at the nearside of the road directly ahead. With experience this reaction becomes second nature, and you start to appreciate oncoming headlights for the extra light which they throw into your path.

The great problem on country roads is that some motorists are too inconsiderate or thoughtless to dip their lights when a motorcyclist approaches, although dipping your own beam in good time usually brings the right response. It is essential to avoid looking directly at main beam lights; instead you must focus your eyes on the nearside of the road ahead, reducing your speed if necessary and keeping a careful eye open for pedestrians and parked vehicles. By all means use a quick flash on to main beam to remind a driver to dip his lights, for this might bring the desired relief to your eyes; but never be tempted to stay on main beam yourself in order to retaliate at a driver who does not respond – having two dazzled road users instead of one doubles the danger. Furthermore, remember how the human eye works: while it can quickly contract the pupil to shut out unwanted light, it takes much longer to dilate afterwards. For several risky seconds after the other vehicle has passed you may be riding in a semi-dazzled state.

It is essential to remember that basic rule of good motorcycling – always travel at a speed which enables you to stop within the distance you can see – when riding at night. This means keeping your speed down so that you can always pull up within the distance illuminated by your headlight. On dipped beam along a straight road this may mean that your speed has to be lower at night than during the day. When changing from main to dipped beam,

Motorcyclists need to ensure that they are seen by other road users. In many accidents involving cars, the driver claims that he simply never spotted the rider. In the first picture (top) the unlit machine is comparatively inconspicuous. The second picture (centre) underlines how much more easily seen a motorcycle is with the headlamp on, even in daylight, and even more so if the full beam (bottom) is used.

reduce your speed if necessary to a level appropriate to your shorter range of visibility.

You need to be aware constantly of the state of the road surface. This means riding on main beam whenever you are on an empty road, although the concentration of light from dipped beam can be preferable to pick out the nearside of the road when rounding left-hand bends. Be very cautious when the road surface is bad, and remember that the central position of a motorcycle headlight creates a temptation to ride directly at a suspicious object or patch of road to illuminate it better.

Approaching lights can give warning of bends and converging roads, but be careful of the difficulty of judging the distance and speed of oncoming vehicles. The brightness of a pair of lights and the fact that little is visible between them mean that an approaching vehicle can be very much closer and travelling more quickly than you think. Advanced motorcyclists, needless to say, must apply the fullest concentration and most careful observation before deciding to overtake at night.

It is just as vital that your headlight is used to help you to be seen. Do not join that curious breed of British drivers who think that dipped headlights should be used with the greatest reluctance, and that parking lights are perfectly adequate for driving around town. Always use your dipped headlight, day and night, town and country, to emphasise your presence to other road users. In bad weather or towards dusk, your headlight is particularly valuable in helping others to judge the speed of your approach, for a motorcycle becomes practically invisible in such conditions when running without lights or on pilot light only. The message is the same when riding in built-up areas at night; your dipped headlight makes you more conspicuous and helps you to pick up road surface abnormalities which might not be revealed by the uneven light cast by street lights.

Make sure that you are completely familiar with the light switches on your machine. Going from main beam to complete blackness at 60mph while fumbling with the dip and on-off switches is an unpleasant experience which can be avoided by keeping the appropriate thumb in practice. This action needs to be completely automatic, even in cold weather, so that your concentration can be kept fully on the road.

Be sure to keep your headlight clean to make the most of the illumination, for even a thin film of grime can cut the light output by half, while only a tenth may get through a thick layer. On damp winter roads it is surprising how quickly mud can coat your headlight; just think how often you need to clean your goggles or visor, and then imagine the layer of dirt which your headlight is trying to pierce. If conditions are particularly mucky, therefore, wipe down the lens whenever you need to clean your visor or goggles.

Summary

- Always be sure that all your *lights are working*, and that your headlight is correctly adjusted.
- Stop for *regular breaks* when making a long journey at night. *Fatigue* is very dangerous; when you begin to feel drowsy your concentration and speed of reaction suffer.
- Use *dipped* and *main beam* intelligently, and make sure that you can always stop safely in the distance illuminated by your headlight.
- Ride with your *dipped headlight* illuminated all the time – day and night, town and country – so that you are seen. Make sure that all your lights, particularly the headlight, are kept clean.
- Be aware of the difficulties of *judging distance* at night, particularly when overtaking.

16

SEASONAL VARIATIONS

Motorcycling in winter and summer weather conditions can present its own special difficulties. Although British winters are mild most of the time, rain and strong winds mean that the motorcyclist often has to take account of the elements, while a cold snap makes roads very treacherous. Summer can sometimes throw up freak bouts of weather which also require extra care.

Riding in winter

Wet roads
The slippery road surfaces and poor visibility caused by rain are the most common problems for the motorcyclist in winter. Constant caution and sensitive use of the controls are required: corners should be taken more slowly to prevent skidding and braking should be gentle, with the emphasis on the rear brake and the engine's retarding effect. Try to keep well clear of other vehicles, especially when speeds rise; cars tend to mist up in bad weather and the way drivers concentrate on the view ahead can make them less attentive to motorcycles behind or to either side. In addition, the spray of muddy water thrown up by vehicles makes judging speed and distance more difficult.

Spray also coats your goggles or visor, either of which are prone to misting up on the inside in winter weather; this can be prevented by applying one of the anti-mist compounds available from accessory shops or by rubbing the lens with washing-up liquid. Whichever method you hoose, always be careful to keep your goggles or visor lear, even if this means stopping by the roadside to do a horough job.

cy roads

Beyond the hazards presented by rain, the motorcyclist lso has to cope with freezing conditions in winter. Here here are no tricks you can use – just common sense. It is ital to understand the conditions, and read the road so hat you anticipate dangerous spots before they catch you ut. Frost is heaviest through the night and in the early norning, so the risks are reduced in cold weather if you an make a journey during the middle of the day. Try to eep to main roads which have been salted and gritted, nd to an extent scoured by traffic, since minor roads may ot have been treated in the same way. An indirect result f gritting is that the fine layer of gravel deposited on the oad is soon worked towards the verge by passing traffic, naking it a good idea to ride consistently a few feet further ut from the kerb, where the surface will be drier and nore solid.

Even on a fine day when the road surface seems normal, be aware that ice might have remained where rees and walls shade the road, where gradients are not varmed by the sun, or where wind sweeps across an xposed hilltop or bridge. Although the roughened texture f many concrete road surfaces with grooves running aterally across the road can offer good grip in dry veather, the water which settles in the grooves can create a very treacherous surface when it freezes. Expert bservation of the road surface is crucial when dealing vith isolated patches of frozen road, but keep an eye on ther road users as well since their actions can give you dvance warning of danger.

Black ice

The notorious hazard of black ice should always be expected on a cold night, and for several hours on the following morning. Black ice occurs where water has melted during the day, spread across the road and then frozen again as the temperature drops after dusk, creating a surface that is like a well-greased ice rink. The danger is

that you may think the surface of the road illuminated by
your headlight appears to be wet, when in fact it is icy – on
some road surfaces it can be virtually invisible. Because it
occurs in patches, it is very easy to be lulled into a sense of
false security after riding for several miles along a road
which seems normal. The only advice must be to ride very,
very gingerly when the temperature is low enough for
black ice to be a risk.

Bike maintenance
It is vital that your motorcycle is in good shape to carry you
through the winter, whether you do the servicing yourself
or have it done by a dealer. If you do your own
maintenance but have no garage, avoid skimping on
attention just because it is unpleasant to work outside on a
cold day; at least this is preferable to a breakdown in rain
or on a cold night far from home. Grip is your first priority
in winter, so make sure that your tyres have plenty of
tread, no sidewall damage and no 'flat spots' caused by
skidding; pressures should be checked regularly.

Electrical systems are tested severely in winter.
Batteries or magnetos must be in good condition to cope
with starting on cold mornings, and the short daylight
hours mean that heavy demands are made on lighting
systems. Wiring, bulb-holders (bad earth connections can
cause trouble here) and generators should all be checked.
Since it can be difficult to diagnose faults in the generator
and its control system, it is a good idea to have these parts
checked by an electrical specialist before winter draws in.

Damp plug leads and connectors can often cause
uneven engine running during winter, since water can
work its way under connectors to short out spark plugs
during heavy rain, this dampness lingering for days
afterwards to cause intermittent misfiring. The answer is
to fit connectors with good waterproof seals at both ends of
the plug leads, and to keep an eye on plug gaps and
cleanliness. A dirty plug with the gap out of adjustment will
often miss a spark, and then cease to work altogether
when dampness prevents the current from reaching it.
Check the condition of plug leads, looking for any signs of
cracking in the insulation or heat damage caused by
contact with the cylinder fins or exhaust pipe. Looking

over the leads in darkness, with the bike on its stand and the engine running, can show current leaks more clearly.

Corrosion

Corrosion during the winter is a problem best prevented by frequent washing down to remove the salt and road dirt which cause steel and iron to rust and alloy to deteriorate through oxidation; chrome can be preserved by treating it with a proprietary cleaner and paintwork benefits from regular waxing. Some motorcyclists like to coat wheels, engine castings and parts of the frame with grease or vaseline to repel salt and water, and then clean off this protective – but messy – layer with solvent when spring comes. An owner without a garage might consider buying a plastic cover from an accessory shop, but do not expect too much in the way of protection from one of these as condensation can form inside if there are no holes to allow ventilation. Even if a wet machine is wiped down before being covered it can be damp again within hours, this moisture remaining long after the weather has brightened up. A plastic cover gives some protection, but is no substitute for regular cleaning.

Dealing with frost

Very low overnight temperatures can cause small difficulties even with the most fastidiously maintained machine. Frozen fork or ignition locks can be thawed by heating the keys with a match, although keeping locks lubricated with a drop of light oil is a good preventive measure. Some lock experts frown on this because oil collects dirt, but it certainly prevents water from getting in. Sluggish starting on cold mornings can often be overcome by kicking over the engine gently a few times before using a stronger kick or the electric starter, and a light kick with the clutch lever depressed will make sure that oil-bath clutches do not stick and stall the engine when you try to move off.

Towing

If you do suffer a breakdown during a winter journey, a tow may be necessary if the problem cannot be cured at the roadside. In this eventuality remember that a special technique is needed for towing a motorcycle: never tie the rope to the motorcycle frame, but loop it carefully around the handlebars so that you can hold on to the free end with your left hand. As well as giving you more freedom in using the brakes, in an emergency this allows you to release the end so that the bike is not dragged along the ground. Remember that a solo motorcycle can be towed legally only by another motorcyle.

Suitable clothing

The cold and damp weather of winter is just as hard on the rider as it is on the machine. As well as making sure that your protective clothing keeps you warm enough (see Chapter 23), build in enough time on a long journey to make frequent stops to warm up and stretch cold limbs. It is impossible to work the controls quickly and sensitively in an emergency if your hands and feet are numb with cold, and this coldness soon exhausts your whole body, slowing down your reactions and impairing concentration.

Fairings

Many experienced motorcyclists recognise the value of a fairing to divert cold air, rain and spray. Although many people think that a fairing is also an aid to speed, this is really only true at racing speeds. Many independent tests have shown that fairings – either of sports or touring styles – make surprisingly little difference to acceleration, speed or fuel consumption at legal road speeds, for anything gained by improved airflow is largely cancelled out by extra weight and increased frontal area. Instead, the advantage of a fairing is the greater comfort it provides, especially in winter.

If you feel that you would benefit from a fairing there are also disadvantages which need to be investigated before you decide to buy one. Although the disadvantages vary with the machine and type of fairing, possible problems include reduced steering lock and fitting difficulties, the latter perhaps involving repositioning of instruments, handlebars, controls, headlight shells, wiring and indicators. It would be a good idea to try to borrow a bike fitted with the fairing you like so that you can assess whether the increased comfort (particularly in the rain) is worth the expenditure. If you plan to fit a fairing yourself make sure you find out exactly how difficult the job might be, for the salesman might play down the problems. Although inevitably you will be influenced by style in choosing a fairing, do pay attention to the functional advantages; many sports fairings look exciting but fail to give much protection to the rider's hands.

Riding in summer

After the perils of riding in winter, all motorcyclists perk up at the thought of the dry roads, long hours of daylight, good visibility and warm air which come with summer, even a typically mediocre British one. It is as well to remember, though, that summer can present problems too, even if they are minor compared with those of winter.

Slippery roads

One of the most important aspects which needs to be remembered about summer riding is that a film of dust, rubber and oil accumulates on road surfaces during dry weather. While this does not greatly affect the grip of your tyres while the road remains dry, a summer shower or morning dew can make this greasy coating almost as slippery as ice. The longer a spell without rain, the more treacherous the roads can be when rain does come, particularly at points where traffic is heavy. Make sure that you are always aware of this phenomenon, but pay particular attention at roundabouts, junctions, in towns and through bends on roads where traffic is heavy. After a while this coating is washed away by rain so that the surface becomes less slippery, but take it easy all the time.

Overheated roads

A very hot day when the sun is bright can also cause a road surface to heat up to the point where tarmac begins to melt. Improved road-building techniques have made this problem less marked than it used to be but, even so, a stretch of road where the surface appears to have a sheen may well not offer as much grip as usual on a very hot day, particularly if traffic is heavy. Sometimes you see signs of the road surface breaking up on bends under the pressure of heavy lorries, so remember that grip will be reduced on this bumpy, slightly molten surface.

Loose chippings

Summer is the time when many local authorities, seemingly with increasing frequency, decide to dress their roads with a layer of tar and stone chippings. Such roads need to be treated circumspectly because grip is greatly reduced and stones are thrown up by vehicles in front. After a while a newly-dressed surface begins to settle down, but even so you should remember that loose stones tend to accumulate at the edge of the road, creating a surface which is akin to riding on marbles.

Summer congestion

You can expect congested roads on holiday routes during school holidays and over bank holiday weekends, and the sun can dazzle a rider who is not equipped with a tinted visor or goggles. The temptation to ride wearing light summer clothing – perhaps just a pair of shorts and a tee-shirt – on a really hot day should be resisted, whatever the cost in personal discomfort. Dressed like this you will have no protection if you suffer a fall from your machine; hot skin is better than no skin at all!

Summer rain

Although it does not usually last long, a summer shower or thunderstorm can be very heavy. Rather than ploughing on in greatly reduced visbility and without the sort of protection offered by winter clothing, it is invariably better to seek shelter until the rain has passed. Rain can fall so quickly that large puddles can form at the edge of the road perhaps where drains are blocked; in this case, slow right down to a pace which allows you to cope if suddenly faced with several inches of water under your wheels. With visibility and tyre adhesion greatly reduced, there is a high risk of falling off your machine, or of a careless car driver running into you. The high humidity which accompanies summer thunderstorms can also make your visor or goggles mist up very quickly, providing another good reason for stopping until the rain abates.

Every now and then rain falls so heavily that roads become flooded in dips, although this occurs more often in winter when the ground is water-logged. Although car drivers might be able to negotiate a flooded road, the risk of unseen potholes and mud makes this unwise for the motorcyclist, apart from the fact that it is easy to become immobilised when water splashed up by the front wheel finds its way into the electrics. If in any doubt, it is much better to turn round and use your sense of direction to find another route along nearby back roads.

If you do decide to press on through water which is only a few inches deep on a road whose visible surface is in good condition, proceed at a modest pace in low gear, taking care to keep the engine revs up to avoid water being sucked back up the exhaust pipe. Keep up an even pace – slipping the clutch if necessary to maintain a good engine speed – which is slow enough to prevent water from the front wheel spraying over the engine. Once clear of the flood, dry the brakes out by riding carefully at low speed with both brakes applied lightly. Speed can be built up after a few hundred yards so that several harder jabs on pedal and lever can finish the job. Since drum brakes take longer than discs to dry, most modern machines will require more application of the rear brake than the front.

Summary

- When roads are slippery in winter or summer, use your bike's controls – brakes, throttle, clutch – even more *smoothly and gently* than normal to avoid the danger of skidding, keeping the emphasis on the rear brake.

- *Read the road* to prepare yourself for slippery spots; treat the surface with the utmost respect if *black ice* seems a possibility.

- Make sure that both you and your motorcycle are *properly prepared* for winter riding; keep visors and goggles clean on the outside and demisted on the inside.

- Bear in mind the hazards of summer riding: allow for *greasy roads* when rain falls after a long dry spell, and take special care when *loose chippings* have been laid as a surface dressing.

- Ride very carefully in the heavy rain of a *summer storm*; visibility can be poor, your visor or goggles may mist up and deep surface water can lie on the road.

17

FOG

While you are most likely to encounter fog during winter, it should be regarded as a hazard which can occur at any time of year. The weather can be misty even in summer, and sea fog is always a possibility on a coastal road. The simple answer to the problem of motorcyling in fog is *don't*, but there will always be occasions, for example if a journey is absolutely essential or you are caught on the road, when you have to ride on. However, if fog is really dense, bear in mind that an unscheduled stop in a hotel is infinitely preferable to a spell in hospital.

Speed and vision

The fundamental rule of riding in fog is that you must keep your speed down to a level which allows you to stop within the range of your vision, even if this means a speed of only 5mph, although such a low speed would probably make it pointless to persevere with your journey. As a motorcyclist, you are in even greater danger in fog than a car driver, so you are asking for trouble if you attempt to ride faster than 'braking distance rate'; you may get away with this for many years but one day you will come a cropper when you collide with something or someone.

Riding at a slow, steady pace, you should use the nearside kerb or verge as the main guide to your position. White lines and cat's eyes can also show you where the road goes, but never let them encourage you into riding faster than your vision allows. Never ride too close to centre lines as you might meet someone in a car or lorry coming in the other direction doing exactly the same thing.

While the limits of vision are a vital consideration, motorcyclists must never forget that fog is usually accompanied by a slippery, damp road surface, so your speed and use of the controls must take account of this.

Your goggles or visor must be kept clean by frequent wiping, as the droplets of water vapour which form fog can accumulate without your noticing it. When riding very slowly in thick fog, it is worth removing your eye protection altogether to give yourself a clearer view.

Being seen

Although we recommend that you always ride with your dipped headlight on, this becomes absolutely vital in fog; never use the pilot light alone as other drivers simply will not be able to spot you as easily. It is better to avoid using main beam, because fog reflects so much light that dipped beam generally gives you a better view. Fog lamps, if you have them, are designed to give better light penetration in fog. Make sure that your rear light is working and that any mud or grime thrown up by the rear wheel is washed off before you start your journey.

Junctions are always hazardous in fog, particularly right turns, so a safe rule is to flash your headlight on to main beam and sound your horn when you have to cross the path of other vehicles which may be hidden in the fog. You are at great risk while turning at a right angle across a road, because your front and rear lights cannot give an oncoming driver advanced warning of your presence; he will be very surprised by the unexpected sight of a motorcyclist crossing his path and his reactions may be slow. Besides all the usual careful observation, try to listen for the sound of an approaching vehicle when about to make a right turn in fog; even with a helmet on you might be able to hear an approaching vehicle before you see it, especially at night.

Traffic

It is very easy to gain the impression in fog that a vehicle ahead of you is moving unnecessarily slowly; remember that while you can see a pair of red beacons through the fog, the driver ahead may be able to see virtually nothing. Never be tempted to overtake, since this puts you – and anyone who might be coming the other way – at great risk. You can also be misled about visibility because a vehicle ahead of you makes a slight 'hole' in the droplets of water vapour which form fog. You may feel that the fog has eased slightly while you are in another vehicle's wake, only to find, when you are committed to an overtaking manoeuvre, that it is as thick as ever. Furthermore you may feel under pressure, once you are in front, to justify your manoeuvre to drivers pressing close behind by riding too fast for the conditions. Instead, it is much better to keep station and control any impatience caused by the vehicle ahead moving very slowly.

While it is wise to stay in line, do not be tempted to stay in touch with the tail lights of a driver whose speed seems too fast for safety. In the sense of loneliness which accompanies fog it can be reassuring to ride in the presence of other vehicles, giving your eyes some relief from the strain of peering through the gloom, but do so only in a manner which is safe for the conditions. When you are following another vehicle, leave enough space to stop, remembering that the driver may not slow down and stop in the normal way. There is always the risk that the leader of a convoy will hit a crashed car and stop instantaneously. The result of such nose-to-tail travelling can be catastrophic for everyone involved, but the motorcyclist sandwiched between cars and lorries is in the greatest danger.

As a motorcyclist you ought to have developed such a sense of your own vulnerability that you automatically maintain a safe speed and distance, but car drivers are notorious for travelling too fast and too close together in fog. If a driver overtakes and fills the space you have left, you must just ease back for a moment to restore the correct distance. You can discourage motorists from squeezing past you by riding well out into the road, since having a car ahead to act as a 'pilot' reduces the need for you to use the nearside verge as a guide to your position. But do not impede the progress of an impetuous driver who clearly wishes to pass; let him by and then stay well out of his way.

Publicity is centred on motorway accidents in fog because they are so serious, but there is no reason why motorways should not be safer in fog, just as they are in normal weather conditions. Accidents would rarely occur if everyone observed the simple rule about 'braking distance rate', instead of rushing blindly into the fog at high speed just because they know traffic will not be coming the other way. You must look after yourself by riding safely and attentively, ignoring the fools who blast by. Illuminated motorway warning signals always post a temporary maximum speed when it is foggy, but follow your own judgement if you feel that the speed indicated is too fast. The best policy of all for the motorcyclist is simply to leave the motorway at the next exit and take an alternative trunk road route.

So far we have dealt only with the fairly continuous fog which usually occurs in winter, but you must remember that fog can occur in patches, sometimes when you least expect it. Pockets of fog can linger in valleys on an undulating country road – even in summer if the humidity, temperature and air currents are right; alternatively, high ground can be foggy on a very overcast day. Fog tends to form first over water; if you see mist developing, expect thicker patches where the road crosses a river. You can imagine the danger if you are travelling at 60mph when you hit a patch of thick fog, so be prepared for it if you see any signs of mist over the surrounding landscape. Take the usual precautions when the mist does appear: drop your speed, make sure that your dipped headlight is on and keep a sharp eye open for any slow-moving or stationary vehicles already involved in a collision.

Summary

- The golden rule in fog is to *reduce your speed* so that you can stop within the *range of your vision*, even if this means that you ride at only 5mph. Consider postponing or abandoning a journey if conditions are very bad.
- Always use your *dipped headlight*, day or night; remember that fog makes the road surface damp and coats your visor or goggles with moisture.
- Take a sensible attitude in traffic: *do not overtake*, because you may have been misled about the visibility

when riding behind another vehicle; do not stay in touch with a driver who is *travelling too fast*; always allow enough space so that you can stop safely if the vehicle ahead *stops instantaneously* in a collision.

18

REACTION TIMES

Throughout this book we refer to the importance of *anticipating* the actions and movements of others, and of reducing your own speed to allow for the possibility of heavy braking or a sudden change of course. As well as allowing for what another road user might do, it is necessary also to have some idea of how long it will take him to react, and how long you will need to take any appropriate action. While riding you must be familiar with the effect of reaction times on your own actions and those of others.

Your reactions

Reaction times vary widely from person to person, and are invariably longer than you might think. A professional racing motorcyclist who is physically fit, gifted in high-speed riding, blessed with naturally fast reactions and fired with adrenalin can react remarkably quickly, in as little as 0.2 of a second. This represents the time which elapses between the rider recognising a hazard and the beginning of his action – whether applying the brakes, accelerating or changing course. If you consider that it takes about a second to say 'one thousand', you begin to understand the lightning speed of a racing motorcyclist's reactions: in one-fifth of a second he can recognise a hazard, decide on the degree of danger, assess what might happen next, choose a course of action and then act on it.

The average rider is much slower to react: 0.4 of a second is excellent, 0.5 is still good and 0.8 is satisfactory. Anything longer than a second is definitely getting dangerously slow. To gain a rough idea of your reaction time you can go to a driving centre equipped with a simulation tester: you sit at the simulated controls of a car and have to brake when a hazard, or just a 'brake' warning, flashes on the screen in front of you. As a very unscientific alternative, the party game which involves gripping a pencil or long piece of card which someone drops between your thumb and forefinger can show how your reactions compare with those of other people.

Remember that the speed of your reactions can vary considerably; they slow down if you are tired, ill or under stress. If you have to ride when you are feeling at all below par, you must take this into account. Your reaction time might be 0.5 of a second when you are fit, but when you have a heavy cold or influenza it could increase to 0.8 of a second. That extra 0.3 makes a tremendous difference to the distance you travel before you start to take avoiding action for a hazard ahead. Keeping warm, with adequate protective clothing and frequent stops to restore circulation, also helps to prevent your reaction time deteriorating when riding in winter. Frozen hands and a numbed brain can slow down your reaction time to the point where fumbling fingers reach the controls only *after* an accident has occurred.

The table overleaf shows the distance travelled for three different reaction times at various speeds. For the sake of safety, assume that your reaction time is on the slow side, say 0.9 of a second, and allow for this in the semi-instinctive calculations you make on the road when judging braking distance, an overtaking manoeuvre and so on.

You should, of course, reduce the effect of your reaction time by reading the road ahead and realising when and where a hazard might occur. If you suspect that potential danger lies ahead, it is always wise to open the hand from the throttle grip and hold your fingers poised over the front brake lever. This anticipation will save a valuable tenth or so of a second while your brain passes a 'release throttle and operate brakes' message to your right hand and left foot. There may be occasions, too, when you take the precaution of selecting a lower gear so that you are ready for instant acceleration away from danger.

You must allow more reaction time at night because your eyes have to adjust constantly to changing levels of light. The pupil of the eye contracts quickly to adjust your vision when bright headlights approach, but it takes much

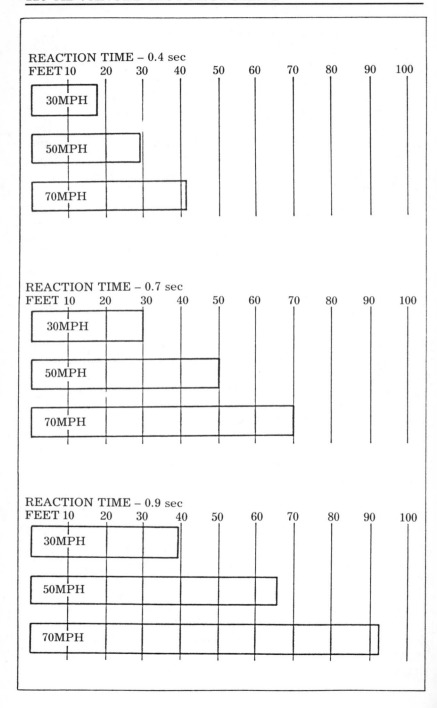

longer to adapt to darkness again once the lights have gone; while your eyes adjust back you are riding with temporarily impaired vision. During these moments, when it is difficult to see what lies ahead, the time you need to recognise developments which may affect you will increase. The care needed to allow for this was discussed in Chapter 15; since your reaction time can rise to several seconds, reduce your speed accordingly.

Other people's reactions

While you can take a little positive action to allow for the effect of your own reaction time, nothing can be done about the shortcomings of road users around you other than always to expect slow reactions. Remember that car and lorry drivers tend to have slightly slower reactions because their feet and hands have further to move from accelerator to brake pedal, and from steering wheel to gear lever.

It is common for a rider involved in an accident with a four-wheeler to complain that the driver 'had plenty of time to see me', and maybe by the aggrieved rider's standards he did. But you cannot take for granted sharp reactions – or fail-safe observation – in another road user. An incident where a motorcyclist collides with a car because its driver pulls too slowly across the rider's path could, in some circumstances, be blamed on both parties; the motorcyclist is wrong to assume that the driver has quick reactions and should allow room for his hesitant approach.

Two popular myths must be dealt with before we leave the subject of reaction times. The first is the view (thankfully now rejected by the vast majority of motorcyclists and drivers) that alcohol speeds up reactions. Drinking has precisely the *opposite* effect, for it dulls the nervous system so that you react more slowly to outside influences. The problem is that judgement diminishes under the influence of alcohol, so that some people *think* that they can react more quickly after a few drinks. Of course, this is complete rubbish: you should never drink and ride a motorcycle. Remember too that drugs can slow you down, so when you are given a prescription ask your doctor if it is safe to ride: anti-histamines (for hay fever sufferers) and tranquillisers are two common drugs which might cause drowsiness. You should ask about any pills you may buy from a chemist: anti-sickness tablets, for example, can have side effects which are disastrous when you are riding.

The second myth is that familiar claim from drivers or riders involved in an accident: 'I stopped dead'. Now that you know just how far you can travel while you are reacting to a hazard, you can see that this statement is daft. Besides, no motorcycle can ever stop 'dead': if it could, you certainly would not stop with it . . .

Summary

- Never underestimate your *reaction time*, or the distance your bike can travel while you are reacting.
- Allow for the fact that your reaction time increases when you are *below par*: feeling unwell, cold, sleepy or stressed can all affect your riding dramatically.
- Do not assume that *other road users* will react as quickly as you expect them to.

19

ACCIDENTS

Every motorcyclist hopes never to be involved in an accident, but the chances of avoiding one throughout your riding life are statistically quite small – even for an advanced motorcyclist. It is worth taking a little trouble, therefore, to make sure that you know what to do if the worst does occur. At the same time you are very likely, sooner or later, to arrive at the scene of someone else's accident, and if you are one of the first to arrive it will be your responsibility to help. The advice which follows on what to do is from the Metropolitan Police.

Stop and think

Many things have to be done at once at an accident, and there is more involved than merely helping the casualties. You must warn other drivers, send for help, and protect the site from further accidents until the emergency services arrive. Your actions in these first few minutes could be a matter of life and death. Think about what you do: someone who is injured and unable to move could be more seriously hurt if you try to pull him out of a crashed car.

Park safely

Do not park your motorcycle where it could be a hazard to other traffic. The best place to park is at the roadside between the accident site and oncoming traffic where your machine can be seen easily. When it is dark, position your bike so that its headlight illuminates the scene of the accident, but also so that it can still be seen by approaching drivers. Switch off the crashed vehicle's engine and disconnect the battery; apply the handbrake and chock the wheels if this seems necessary. Make sure that no-one in the vicinity of the accident is smoking.

Warn other road users

Approaching drivers need plenty of time and distance in which to react to warning signals, and to slow down and stop or negotiate the accident. Running into the road and waving your arms wildly will confuse others and put yourself in danger. Instead, walk back along the side of the road for at least 100 yards, or until the accident is going out of view. Make a clear 'slow down' signal by moving your arm vigorously up and down, with palm face down, as if pressing down repeatedly on a heavy weight, and point decisively to the accident scene. On bends it may be useful to recruit a second person to give advance warning.

Someone should stand near the site and guide vehicles round the accident. Stand in the headlights of a car or under a streetlamp at night, and remember that it will help to wear a pale or reflective garment. Hold a white handkerchief, or better still a torch, in your hand to draw extra attention to yourself. If you can find a driver who carries an advance warning sign (a red reflective triangle), place it in the road at least 50 yards (150 yards on a motorway) before the accident and on the same side of the road to warn approaching traffic of the obstruction.

Send for help

Your first priority is to send for help, because you will need it! If this means leaving casualties unattended, get someone else to telephone the emergency services. If no-one else is around you must do this yourself.

Answer these questions

These questions must be answered before leaving the accident scene to telephone for the emergency services. What is the *exact* location? (Look for an obvious landmark if you do not know, or if there are no road signs.) How many casualties are there and how serious are their injuries? Are the casualties trapped? Is the accident causing danger? Is a traffic jam developing? Are petrol or chemicals spilling? How many vehicles are involved? Are they cars? Lorries? Tankers? Buses or coaches?

Dial 999

Tell the operator your telephone number and ask for ambulance, police or fire brigade; you will be connected to each in turn if all three are required, Ask for:

Ambulance   if there are casualties.

Police   if there are casualties, danger or obstruction to traffic,

Fire brigade if there are people trapped, petrol or chemicals on the road, or risk of fire.

Give this information

Details which should be given to the emergency services are: exact location of the accident; number and general condition of the casualties; if anyone is trapped; number and type of vehicles involved; if petrol or chemicals are on the road; if other traffic is in danger of jamming up; your name and address, and the telephone number from which you are speaking.

Then return to the accident scene to help with the casualties or traffic. If you saw what happened, give your name and address to the attending police officer. Try to avoid leaving the scene of the accident before speaking to the police but if you do, you should contact any police station or officer as soon as possible to give details.

If an accident occurs involving only slight damage to vehicles and no offence has been committed, it is not necessary to report it to the police. The drivers or riders involved, however, are required by law to exchange details of name and address, vehicle owner and vehicle registration number. If injury is caused you must also give your insurance particulars. Anyone requiring advice or assistance may telephone the local police station or, in an emergency, dial 999.

Help the casualties

Only move injured people if there is immediate danger, since you could aggravate internal and back or neck injuries. Make sure the person can breathe. Inspect the inside of the mouth and back of the throat. To avoid the danger of choking, remove any food, sweets or false teeth. Listen, and if you cannot detect any breathing, try to restore the casualty by mouth-to-mouth resuscitation.

Place the casualty on his back, and support the neck so that the head falls back to open the airway. Pinch his nose shut and hold his mouth open. Cover his mouth with yours, and blow out firmly to inflate his lungs. Then release nose and mouth. Keep repeating the procedure until the casualty starts to breathe spontaneously. If he is unconscious, move him gently into the recovery position to make sure that he does not choke on his tongue or gorge. This involves turning the casualty gently on his side and bending his arms and legs so as to keep him in the position shown in the accompanying diagram. Straighten and turn his head to one side, facing slightly downwards.

If there is serious bleeding, apply firm pressure to the bleeding point to stem the flow of blood. Use a pad or apply a sterile dressing and bandage firmly. Look for limb fractures and try to stop these limbs moving. If a casualty is sitting up and in no immediate danger, do not make him leave the car. Leave him where he is and support his head in case he passes out and chokes.

Keep all casualties warm, including shock cases, but do not give them any pain relievers, alcohol, other drinks, food or cigarettes – they may have internal injuries and need operations.

If you are not sure what to do, leave well alone provided that the casualty is breathing and not bleeding heavily.

The recovery position (top) *and the kiss of life. Their application is described above.*

Get first aid training

This chapter gives only the most elementary first aid advice, but if you have been trained in first aid you will clearly be able to help more effectively. The British Red Cross Society or the St John Ambulance Association can advise you about training.

Carry a first aid kit

By carrying a first aid kit you are better prepared to help yourself and other road users in the event of an accident, it may even save someone's life. Your first aid kit should be clearly marked and easily accessible, and can be carried in any suitable plastic container, preferably a flexible and transparent one. Mark it 'First Aid' or paint a large red cross on it.

This box should contain plenty of sterile dressings – as many as can be fitted in – in large, medium and small sizes. Triangular bandages for use as slings or bandages, safety pins, plasters, scissors and a knife are essential. You could carry anti-sting and scald ointments for minor mishaps which might impair your riding, but these should not be used in accidents. Do not carry antiseptics, pain-relieving pills or alcohol, as all of these can do more harm than good on the road.

(*The Institute's thanks go to the Metropolitan Police for the above advice.*)

Fire

There is just one set of circumstances at the scene of an accident when you should break the rule and pull injured people from their vehicles. Although fire occurs in only a tiny proportion of road accidents, it is a very serious hazard which requires instant action and great presence of mind. The fire may be caused by a short circuit from damaged wiring, in which case you should have plenty of time to deal with it as long as petrol is not seeping from a ruptured tank dangerously near it. If one of the crashed vehicles carries a fire extinguisher, aim it at the seat of the fire and keep up the discharge until the flames are out.

If the fire is in the engine bay, great care is needed since the action of opening the bonnet will feed the fire with a draught of air, causing the flames to flare up. If you can, open the bonnet just enough to allow you to aim the fire extinguisher inside, *but only if you can identify with certainty the source of the flames*. If you cannot see where the fire is coming from before you open the bonnet a fraction, open it wide and be ready to act quickly if the fire expands. If you can, try to break the electrical circuit feeding the fire by disconnecting the battery leads.

A petrol fire is even more serious, calling for heroic action if anything is to be done to save people trapped inside the car. A petrol fire can often be avoided, however, by making sure that there is no possibility of any sparks near the damaged car; no-one must smoke, people in nailed shoes should keep clear and no attempt should be made by anyone but the emergency services to cut away metal to release occupants. Petrol cannot set itself alight, so one of your first actions must be to switch off the car's ignition to avoid the possibility of any sparks.

Accident procedures

The majority of accidents are no more than minor collisions involving bumps and scrapes to vehicles or motorcycles and no injury to people, but even these should be treated seriously. The law demands that you give your name and address and insurance company details to the other driver and to anyone else, such as a police officer, who may reasonably require it. It is your responsibility to make sure that you obtain these same details from the other driver. Remember to collect information from any other motorists or pedestrians who saw the incident, but be quick about it because witnesses, realising they might have to waste a day in court on your behalf, have a habit of melting away into the background.

You are not required by law to inform the police if all these points are followed, but it is always advisable to do so if anyone is injured or there is an allegation of dangerous driving. Many people think that causing damage to a parked vehicle, perhaps by scratching a handlebar lever along its wing, is part of the rough and tumble of life, but it is unethical – and illegal – to ride off without leaving a note of your name and address under the windscreen wiper.

Severe collisions

In collisions where more severe damage is caused to vehicles, it is best to leave them where they come to rest until the police have inspected the incident and taken measurements. Take photographs if you happen to be carrying a camera, because they could be very useful as evidence if the matter should ever come before a court. Take your own measurements and make notes of exactly what happened so that you can give very precise information to your insurance company. The more detail you can provide, the better the chance, if the incident was someone else's fault, that his company and not yours will be paying up.

Take care not to say anything, either to the other driver or to the police, which you may later regret. It is always possible that you may say things in the heat of the moment which may subsequently be interpreted as acceptance by you of liability. Think carefully before you speak even if you do accept that you were at fault; every insurer advises that you should leave the assessment of blame to them and not admit it on the spot.

Minor collisions

Very minor collisions causing only superficial damage may result in a great deal of anger, but sometimes it is better to be philosophical if the incident is not your fault, and put the cost down to bad luck. On a busy road, other road users will not thank you for causing a traffic jam while you argue over a bent foot-rest. The police also would not be pleased about being dragged into such an inconsequential matter which would hardly merit prosecution. You may be fortunate in finding that the offending motorist agrees to pay for your minor repairs himself but, if he does not, you are unlikely to be able to persuade his insurance company to pay. They would know that the cost, time and trouble of legal action would never be worthwhile to extract a small amount of money, and you would hardly want to go to your own insurer with a claim which would probably be exceeded by the cost of higher premiums in the future.

However annoying it may be at the time, you may have to put a minor knock down to experience.

'Hit and run' incidents
If ever you see a 'hit and run' accident, try to absorb as many details as you can and write them down as soon as possible – registration number, colour and make of the vehicle involved, a description of the incident and maybe even a description of the driver. The more details you can pass to the police, the better chance they have of tracing the culprit. Do not forget, though, that your first duty is to the victim.

Protecting yourself

Although the question of protective clothing is dealt with in Chapter 23, no discussion of accidents involving motorcycles would be complete without some mention of this vital point. Research has shown that 85 per cent of accidents resulting in injury to motorcyclists involve frontal or near-frontal impacts in which the rider is usually thrown off.

Conventional wisdom has always suggested that a motorcyclist about to have an accident should 'step off' his machine, since the chances of escaping serious injury are better if you are sliding along the road surface rather than rolling with the bike likely to land on top of you. Whether you fling yourself off deliberately or are thrown clear of the machine, scraping along the road will certainly cause minor injuries unless you are well protected. The legal obligation to wear a helmet means that your head is looked after, but hands, feet, arms and legs are very vulnerable, especially if you land awkwardly. However warm the weather, you need to wear gloves, boots and a tough jacket as a minimum to prevent the gashes and grazes which experts call 'nuisance injuries', although the word 'nuisance' hardly fits with the pain and inconvenience which they cause. While you work to develop the skills of advanced riding to a level which ensures that you will never be involved in an accident, do recognise that you need to be dressed for protection should you have one.

Summary

- Absorb carefully the details contained in this chapter about *accident procedure* when you are one of the first on the scene: in this eventuality you must act swiftly and with great presence of mind.
- Carry a *first aid kit* and make sure that you know how to use it.
- At minor accidents which involve no injury, your *exchange of details* with the other party should include names and addresses, vehicle details and names of insurance companies; do not admit liability even if you feel that you were at fault.

20

PILLION PASSENGERS AND SIDECARS

Most motorcyclists spend most of their time riding solo, but almost every rider needs sometimes to carry a pillion passenger. It may be just an occasional social outing with a friend, or perhaps a regular commuting run to and from work with a colleague who shares costs. Either way there are special techniques which have to be followed, by the rider as well as his passenger, to make sure that both are safe on the motorcycle. The higher power outputs available from modern motorcycles allow passengers to be carried without too significant an effect on performance, even with smaller capacity bikes. Other riders, perhaps those unwilling to give up the pleasures of motorcycling when they get married and start a family, decide that a sidecar is the answer, and this style of motorcycling also demands special skills.

Pillion passengers

Many experienced motorcyclists have mixed feelings about carrying passengers – riding with a frightened, inexperienced person behind you can be irritating at best and downright dangerous at worst. Passengers with no feel for motorcycling will automatically lean the wrong way to counter the angle when you bank your bike into a corner; they may make sudden movements which will cause the steering to wobble when riding in a straight line; they will grab your waist when accelerating and then slide forwards, pushing you on to the fuel tank, when braking.

After dismounting they may even have the gall to say 'Fun, must do it again', before staggering off to the nearest bar to restore their nerves.

The opposite of these kind of characters are the experienced pillion passengers who have as good a feel as the rider for motorcycling. They will know how to behave unobtrusively and helpfully on the road, and provide the pleasures of good company and shared experiences when a journey is over. The advice which follows should help to turn the first type of pillion passenger into the second, so that you can ride more safely as well as increase your enjoyment of motorcycling by sharing the pleasure.

You must first remind your novice passenger that motorcycling is like riding a bike, telling him that bends are negotiated by leaning the bike over, not by steering the front wheel. Explain that sudden movements affect your control of the bike and that he must keep his body in line with yours at all times, even if he feels uncertain about the angles involved through bends. His feet must always be kept up on the foot-rests, which means resisting firmly the temptation to put his feet down on the ground when the bike is coming to a stop. Tell him that he must not hold you round the waist, as this does not offer him a very secure grip and may pull you off balance. Instead, he should put his hands behind him and hold the 'cissy' bar fitted to most bikes, or the rear edge of the saddle if no bar is fitted. Some bikes have a strap across the centre of the saddle which looks like a tempting hand-hold, but using this is not recommended.

With these basic points covered, you may like to explain that many pillion riders, once they have some experience, rest their hands on their knees and maintain equilibrium with their leg muscles and good body positioning, gripping the rear bar or saddle only when you brake heavily or accelerate briskly. Since wind and engine noise, as well as the constraints of a full-face helmet with its visor down, make it very difficult to communicate verbally when you are on the move, arrange a simple signalling system. Make it clear to the novice that the best way to tell you he wants to stop is with a firm tap on the shoulder.

Before setting off, make sure that your passenger has

the unfamiliar safety helmet fastened securely and comfortably, and ask him to get on the bike after you have mounted so that you can keep things steady and claim a good share of the dual saddle. Check that he is comfortable and has found the foot-rests before you move off. Never accelerate away too quickly, as a newcomer to motorcycling will be far more frightened than impressed if you leave rubber on the road and lift the front wheel in the air – neither will his uneasiness help him to become a good pillion passenger. Even with an experienced person behind you, ride with more restraint than usual and try to avoid sudden changes in speed and course. Remember that your passenger's view of the road ahead will be obscured, giving him little chance to anticipate and prepare himself for sudden movements.

An increasing number of touring enthusiasts find that a rider-to-passenger intercom set, such as a Sonic or Maxon, offers great benefits. As well as being able to talk to the rider on a long journey, the passenger can take on the task of map-reading and route-finding. Intercoms are also a valuable training aid, and experienced IAM observers use them to give demonstration commentary rides to those they are teaching.

Bike-to-bike radio intercom sets can be a mixed blessing, apart from being considerably more expensive. Concern has been expressed about the correct use of vocabulary between riders, so that, for example, 'No' is not misheard as 'Go'. There is also the danger of a less experienced rider being given instructions which may lead him into trouble. If you do decide to invest in bike-to-bike equipment, make sure that you establish clear rules for its use before you take to the road.

Sidecars

As you have probably already discovered, motorcycling is an addictive business; it is hard to give up once you have gained a taste for the habit. The fact that young riders find it difficult to sacrifice their motorcycling if they marry and start a family is the traditional reason for the existence of sidecar combinations. Their determination to continue riding leads them to overlook the inherent design disadvantages of adding a single-wheeled weight to one side of a motorcycle, but many claim to enjoy what has aptly been described as 'doing the impossible with the unrideable'. Although the availability of cheap second-hand cars has all but killed the sidecar, a few sidecar specialists remain to cater for the needs of those who want to stick with motorcycling at all costs. A complete appraisal of the special characteristics of combinations is beyond the scope of this book, but there are some basic points to be made about this difficult aspect of motorcycling.

The geometry of a motorcycle and sidecar is a poor compromise for cornering, since the wheels cannot all follow a constant radius and the wildly uneven weight and power distribution compound the problems. The basic difference involved in riding a motorcycle combination, of course, is that you have to *steer* through corners, not bank through them. The lop-sided weight and power characteristics mean that the basic rule for cornering – assuming that the sidecar is mounted on the left – is to apply power through left-handers (where the sidecar tries to lift off the ground) and remove power through right-handers. The fact that braking encourages the sidecar to overtake the bike (unless the sidecar has its own brake to offset this effect) produces a tendency to turn right, which must be countered by steering gently to the left; acceleration produces an opposite tendency to turn left, which must be countered by steering gently to the right. These characteristics are minimised by paying careful attention to the position of the sidecar wheel in relation to the motorcycle's rear wheel, the attachment point positions, angle of lean, front fork angles and spring travel; even so, the best design will have shortcomings when negotiating a fast, bumpy corner.

While juggling these out-of-balance forces is a skill which can be learned only with practice, you must set yourself off in the right direction by keeping some important factors in mind when considering adding a 'chair' to your machine or buying a combination. Careful choice of bike is essential: many admirable machines have frames which are too weak, engines which lack torque and the wrong fork set-up. Although few in number, sidecar specialists have developed a niche in the market for three-wheels enthusiasts and can give you the advice you need. They know the modifications required for most large-capacity machines – such as BMW K100, Kawasaki GPZ1100 or Yamaha TR1 Vee-twin – to make them suitable.

Once a good match has been achieved, the rider must deliberately forget much of his solo experience and start learning a different set of techniques. He will then be ready to join the small but devoted band of sidecar enthusiasts who enjoy the benefits of extra carrying capacity, lower insurance rates and better performance on slippery surfaces. To see a high-performance sidecar outfit being conducted through a series of fast bends by a good rider is a memorable sight, but such expertise comes only with practice. The relatively high cost incurred in tyres, fuel, chains and sprockets might perhaps compare unfavourably with the economics of running a small car, but the enjoyment outweighs simple logic.

Summary

- Make sure that you give sensible advice to *inexperienced pillion riders* so that they know what to do. A passenger who leans the wrong way, makes sudden movements and slides back and forth with acceleration and braking can impair your control of your machine.
- Even with an experienced passenger, ride with *extra restraint*; try to avoid sudden changes in speed and course.
- Safe handling of a *motorcycle and sidecar* requires practice: absorb the special techniques described here for cornering, braking and accelerating.

21

UNDERSTANDING THE MACHINE

By its very nature, motorcycling generates enthusiasm which leads most riders, regardless of age, type and income, to want to learn how their machines work. After all, if motorcyclists were not so enthusiastic they would probably opt for the greater comfort and ease of travelling by car. A rider's curiosity about his bike's mechanical make-up once would have been forced by the need to deal with frequent breakdowns, but now basic reliability is such an unquestioned quality of all machines, from mopeds to 1000cc superbikes, that mechanical knowledge is no longer a prerequisite for motorcycling. Nevertheless, most riders want to know how their machines work, perhaps so that they can carry out their own servicing; this knowledge helps a rider to handle his bike with more care, consideration and safety as he endeavours to treat the machinery with sympathy and understanding. It is beyond the brief of this book to explore the engineering of a motorcycle in great detail, but there are many books on the subject suitable for everyone from interested layman to qualified engineer. If you count yourself as one of the former, an elementary description of how a motorcycle works might be helpful.

Understanding your motorcycle

The skeleton of every motorcycle is the frame, a structure usually made of steel tubing to which engine, suspension, seat and other components are fastened. In front of the frame, the steering head (attached by a swivel mounting) carries the handlebars on top and a pair of telescopic front forks and the front wheel below. Behind the frame, there

usually a pair of trailing arms which pivot at their front
nds and support the rear wheel at their rear ends.

Both wheels are fitted with a pair of coil springs – the
ont ones inside the forks and the rears usually in the
pen – to insulate the rider from irregularities in the road
nd to keep the wheels pressed firmly in contact with the
urface. Clearly a wheel which is pushed into the air by a
ump cannot give the rider any grip for cornering, braking
r acceleration until the tyre is forced back down on to the
oad. Inside each coil spring is a damper (or shock
bsorber), which moves stiffly in and out to prevent the
pring and wheel continuing to bounce up and down, like a
ubber band with a weight on the end, after passing over a
ump. Various types of brake and operating mechanism
re used to slow down the wheels, but whether discs or
rums are actuated by cable or hydraulic pressure, all rely
n forcing a piece of high-friction material – the brake pad
r lining – on to the metal surface of the disc or drum which
otates with the wheel.

The internal combustion engine used on all
notorcycles works by the expansion effect produced when
mixture of fuel and air is compressed and ignited; the
xpanding gases force the piston downwards, causing the
rankshaft to rotate. The method of introducing the fuel
nixture and removing spent gases is different in two-
troke and four-stroke designs. In a two-stroke, petrol
apour is compressed in the crankcase by the descending
iston until a system of holes and passages in the cylinder
valls allows it to pass into the space above the piston,
orcing out the spent gas and igniting when the piston
ises. In a four-stroke, the piston sucks in petrol vapour
ast a valve in the cylinder head on its first downward
troke, rises to compress this inflammable mixture,
escends again on the power stroke when this mixture is
gnited and then rises to force the exhaust gas through
nother valve ready to start again.

The four-stroke principle (which is used in virtually all
ar engines) produces a cleaner exhaust and greater
moothness, but these engines are more expensive and
omplicated to manufacture. Two-strokes are cheaper to
nake and they produce good power and are simple
nough to be particularly suited to small capacities, but

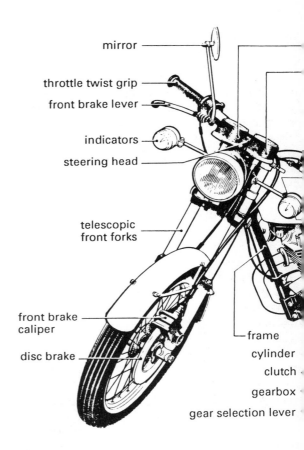

mirror

throttle twist grip

front brake lever

indicators

steering head

telescopic
front forks

front brake
caliper

disc brake

frame

cylinder

clutch

gearbox

gear selection lever

Layout of a typical motorcycle. The details may vary between one model and another, but the basic layout remains unchanged.

rev counter

speedometer

clutch lever

carburettor

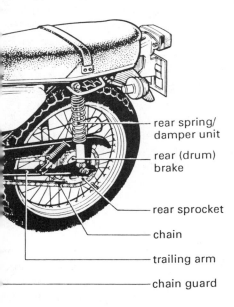

rear spring/
damper unit

rear (drum)
brake

rear sprocket

chain

trailing arm

chain guard

their special lubricating requirements cause more pollution. Whether an engine designer chooses a four-stroke or a two-stroke cycle, he can arrange his engine crankshaft to be driven by one, two, three, four or even six pistons arranged in vee, in-line or horizontally-opposed formations. As a general rule, he is guided by the knowledge that engines with more cyclinders give smoother running and lend themselves to larger capacities but are more expensive and complicated to manufacture.

The engine's crankshaft transmits its power by driving either a gearwheel or endless chain connected through the clutch to the gearbox, and then to the rear wheel either by shaft or by the familiar sprockets and chain. Modern motorcycles have between four and six sets of gear ratios in the transmission to allow the engine to run within its comfortable operating range regardless of how fast the motorcycle is travelling. The clutch can be released so that the engine is disconnected while a different gear is selected or when the bike is standing still.

It is hoped that people with a good understanding of a motorcycle's engineering will forgive this most basic summary, but it may help some readers who have little knowledge of what goes on underneath them when they ride.

Sympathy with your motorcycle

With a clear, if simplified, understanding of how his motorcycle works, the advanced rider will be encouraged to avoid the clumsy or violent use of the controls which puts wear and stress on all mechanical parts. While the techniques of advanced motorcycling to a large extent go hand in hand with mechanical sympathy, it is always wise to remember that insensitive riding hastens the need to spend money on expensive replacement parts.

Making 'Grand Prix getaways' and using full-bore acceleration puts unnecessary strain on all transmission components, stretches the drive chain and sprockets, and wears out the tyres. Leaving your braking to the last moment also increases tyre wear and shortens the life of brake pads and linings. A heavy left foot on the gear-change pedal, together with clumsy use of the clutch, will

orry comes when cornering, since under-inflation allows
e side-walls to move sideways relative to the wheel rim
hen the bike is leaned over. This gives a disconcerting
uirming sensation which feels like the start of a skid;
hen the slack tyre encounters a bump, the side-wall
ovement is accentuated to cause a dangerous wobble.
nder-inflation also causes heat to build up in a tyre,
creasing the rate of wear and leading in extreme
rcumstances to chunks of tread breaking off the tyre
rcass. In addition, soft tyres are more easily damaged
d can increase fuel consumption because more of the
gine's power is absorbed in overcoming tyre resistance.
otorway use quickly reveals even slight under-inflation
 heat builds up in the tyres during continuous riding at
gh speed.

ver-inflation

ver-inflation can occur if an inaccurate pressure gauge is
ed, and results in the tyre bulging in the centre of the
ead pattern so that only a small section is in contact with
e road surface. As much as half of the tyre's grip can be
st, and the central part of the tread will wear rapidly.
ver-inflation also increases the likelihood of bad surfaces
tting the tread rubber and of severe bumps causing
reakage in the cords which form the tyre carcass.

ressure checks

nce the pressure gauges on garage air-lines are often
accurate, it is best for the sake of consistency to use a
nall pocket gauge when making your regular pressure
ecks. Always carry out your check at the start of a trip
hen the air in the tyres is cold; pressure readings are
gher when the air inside the tyres has warmed up. At the
me time inspect the treads for small stones (these can be
rised out with a small electrical-type screwdriver) and the
de-walls for cuts or bulges. If you find that a tyre is slowly
sing pressure, use a little washing-up liquid on the valve
 see if there are any bubbles to indicate a leak; even if
is procedure does not reveal the cause, go to a tyre
ecialist as soon as possible to have the slow puncture
ended before any damage is done to the tyre, or possibly
 you and your bike. Follow the manufacturer's

(a)

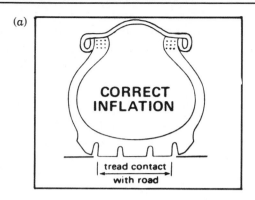

(b)

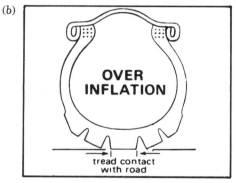

(c)

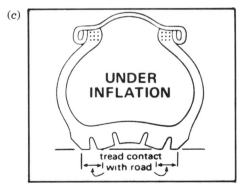

Tyre wear can be minimised by ensuring that pressures are always correct. Correct tyre pressure (a) ensures maximum mileages with satisfactory cushioning, stability and road holding properties. Neither under- nor over-inflation will help tyre grip at all – it will simply make the tyres wear out sooner, destroy the tread pattern and reduce their road grip. Over-inflation (b) makes the centre of the tread wear away, and under-inflation (c) damages the rounded shoulders of the tyre.

recommended pressures as a guide, using your common sense to make slight variations – adding a few pounds to the rear tyre when carrying a pillion passenger for instance – if you feel they are necessary, but do try out the performance immediately through a familiar series of bends: you may feel an unwelcome difference in your bike's handling. Checking the heat of the tyres is also worthwhile, for an increase in temperature is a sure sign of problems.

Wheel balance and alignment
Occasional checks should be made for correct wheel balance, trueness and alignment, as these factors affect tyre wear and road-holding. Any tyre specialist can do this for you, but you can easily do it yourself at home by using simple tools. Trueness can be checked by positioning a steel ruler between a couple of bricks so that the end of the ruler just touches the edge of the wheel rim (with the forks on full lock for the front wheel). Turning the wheel will show whether it is spinning true: the maximum gap between ruler and rim should be 0.06in. Moving the ruler so that it lines up against the centre of the tyre tread and turning the wheel will show if it is 'out-of-round': the maximum gap between ruler and tyre should be 0.04in.

Check wheel balance by spinning the wheel, marking with chalk the lowest point when it stops; spin it several times more, and if the chalk mark repeatedly ends up at the bottom you have found a heavy point. Wrap lead wire (or cored solder) a few inches at a time round the spoke opposite the chalk mark until the wheel can be seen to stop at random after being spun, then secure the wire with tape. Now that cast alloy wheels are more common than the traditional spoked variety, it will be necessary to obtain the adhesive-backed lead weights which tyre specialists use for wheel balancing, or it may be simpler to use their services. Rear-wheel alignment can be checked by laying a straight edge along front and rear rims, any corrections being made with the chain adjusters; remember to correct for any difference between front and rear rim widths.

With wheels and tyres correctly set up, take care not to damage them in use. Scraping against a kerb or banging over one is a common problem which can easily weaken or even break a new tyre's cords. Locking the wheels when braking, spinning the rear wheel under harsh acceleration and scrubbing the treads by cornering too quickly all wear out the tyres more rapidly, and make no appreciable difference to journey times.

Tyre tread
The law requires that tyres should be replaced when tread depth over three-quarters of a tyre's width has worn down to 1mm. This is remarkably lenient, as a tyre's grip in wet weather will have deteriorated considerably by this point; you would be well advised to consider replacement when the tread depth is around 3mm. Other legal requirements cover points obvious to the sensible rider: cords or plies must not be exposed; there should be no lumps or bulges; cuts and breaks in the tread should not be more than 25mm long or 10 per cent of the tyre's width; tyres must be of suitable type and properly inflated; and tread patterns must not be re-cut into old carcasses. Advanced riders should not need the force of law to discourage them from using damaged or worn tyres, since a sense of self-preservation should be sufficient.

Riding with badly worn treads is downright stupid. On a dry road they will offer insufficient grip for emergency action while cornering, and are more prone to puncturing. On a wet surface they are very dangerous, because they provide virtually no grip. Tyre treads are designed to pick up large quantities of water and throw it out behind as the wheels rotate, allowing the rubber to cut through the water and grip on the road surface. This sponging ability is greatly reduced or lost entirely with badly worn treads, causing the tyres to skate along on top of the film of water. Aquaplaning, as this condition is called, will invariably result in an accident, as it will first occur when braking or cornering.

Blow-outs
Modern tyres are so well designed that blow-outs are, mercifully, rare but it is worth outlining how you should react if you are unfortunate enough to suffer this alarming eventuality. You will know about a blow-out quickly enough from your bike's handling, and to stand any

chance of bringing your machine safely to a halt you must apply the brake only on the *good* wheel and steer in a straight line. Veering to one side could roll the flat tyre off the rim, giving you even greater problems. Most punctures, thankfully, are discovered as flat tyres before a bike is taken out on a journey. Whether you remove the wheel and take it to a tyre specialist, or look for your levers to do the job yourself, pause for a moment to consider whether the puncture was merely bad luck, or whether it could have been caused by bad treatment, incorrect pressure or insufficient tread.

Tyre technicalities

When it comes to replacing tyres, you have a huge range from which to choose. In the car market, radial tyres have almost completely superseded the old-fashioned cross-ply types. The advantage to motorists of radials lies in their construction: a radial is made up of cords running parallel to each other, with a strongly reinforced tread around the circumference. This gives the tyre supple side-walls which flex while cornering to leave the tread almost completely flat on the road, giving better grip. Since the tread is not moving around on the surface while cornering, the radial tyre lasts longer than the cross-ply, which has stiffer side-walls owing to its diagonally-laid plies.

For many years it was said that the benefits of radial tyres enjoyed by drivers could not be shared by riders of solo motorcycles. However, tyre designers have been able to meet this challenge so that nowadays several makes of semi-radial and fully-radial motorcycle tyre are available. Nevertheless, a word of caution is necessary: it is absolutely essential to conform to motorcycle manufacturers' recommendations on tyre types. Most radial motorcycle tyres are tubeless, are designed for wide rims and have a low aspect ratio (the ratio of height to width of the tyre's cross-section). These tyres will not fit on rims narrower than those for which they are designed, and any attempt to use a wider tubeless tyre on an unsuitable rim will run the risk of inducing tyre creep and instability; at worst, the tyre can even come off the rim. Provided this advice is followed, there will be very noticeable benefits if your machine will accept radial tyres. Your bike will run more true, it will be less susceptible to 'white-lining', cornering power will be increased, braking ability improved, and there should be at least 20 per cent more mileage compared with the wear rate of a cross-ply.

Whatever type of tyre you choose, it is essential to follow the manufacturer's instructions on tread, size, profile and type. Many tyres are not interchangeable between front and rear wheels, and often the replacement tread will be different from the original. A word about tyre designations is necessary: for a tyre labelled '3.60S18', the first figure refers to the tyre width and the last figure to the wheel rim diameter. The middle letter is the manfuacturer's speed rating needed to comply with European regulations: 'R' means that a tyre is designed for a motorcycle with a maximum speed of 95mph, 'S' for 113mph, 'H' for 130mph and 'V' for over 130mph. The best advice is to stick with the speed rating of your bike's original tyres: they will suit the performance, even if the top speed capability is academic. It is plainly a waste of money to pay for tyres which are designed to go faster than your motorcycle can.

As for choosing between different brands, it is impossible to give definite advice. The advanced rider is likely to select between familiar names like Avon, Michelin, Continental or Dunlop, but Japanese tyres have improved so much that their poor wet-weather reputation is largely a thing of the past. Take advice from tyre specialists and other owners on how different tyres suit your particular machine, and if possible borrow a bike to try out; it has been known for tyres on the same bike to suit one rider's style and not another's. In our view, wet-weather performance is the most important consideration: a tyre which copes well with wet surfaces should be fine in the dry, and it is in wet weather that you really need to be riding on the best rubber available. Once you are sure of this factor, then consider also durability, ride quality and cost. If you choose tubed cross-ply tyres, you would be wise to buy new inner tubes at the same time: the old ones may have stretched, and can crease and possibly puncture when fitted inside new covers.

Once you have new tyres selected and fitted,

remember that the manufacturer's job is over. It is up to you to ensure good performance and long life, which means sensible treatment and regular attention to tyre pressures and condition.

Summary

- Keep a regular eye on *tyre condition* by checking pressures and making sure no damage has occurred. Have your tyres checked by a specialist if you ever have cause to believe that you might have damaged them.
- A motorcycle is extremely dangerous on *worn tyres* in all conditions, and lethal in wet weather.
- When buying *new tyres*, whether cross-ply, semi-radial or radial, make sure that they will suit your machine and riding style: wet-weather performance should be your top consideration.

23

CLOTHING

Motorcyclists had little choice in the past when it came to clothing, and most used to finish up in drab outfits assembled at a local government surplus store. These clothes may have been cheap but they were poor value, compared with today's huge selection of suits, trousers and jackets, when it came to providing the four main qualities which motorcycling clothes must possess: they must keep the rider warm, dry, conspicuous and protected in the event of an accident. All this must be achieved without causing any discomfort or impairing ability to operate the controls.

The need for good clothing

To achieve these objectives of warmth, waterproofing, visibility and protection, the motorcyclist must make some sacrifices:

- Time: waterproofing and warmth require many zips, studs, flaps and straps.
- Style: although motorcycling clothes can look good nowadays, they will always appear rather inelegant to anyone but a fellow motorcycling enthusiast.
- Money: effective clothing is usually costly, so allowance must be made for this expenditure when first assessing the costs of buying and using a motorcycle.

When considering the question of clothing, every rider seeks the same comfort and safety. As there are so many different ways of fulfilling this aim, however, your type of use needs to be your first thought. If you tend to cover short distances on a motorcycle or moped equipped with a fairing, the good protection already offered by leg shields and windscreen will mean that a lightweight anorak or oversuit should be quite adequate. At the other end of the scale, long winter journeys on a large capacity superbike will be covered most comfortably in three layers of clothing: a top layer to keep out water, a second to keep you warm and a third to give protection in an accident.

Most riders can happily settle for less expensive and elaborate clothing for everyday use, but may need an outfit which is good enough to get them through an occasional winter cross-country trip. While we can make suggestions, everyone has different views on how this can be achieved. In working out the compromise which suits you, you will want clothes which will be comfortable in summer yet will also contribute in the effort to combat winter conditions. The best advice we can give is first to obtain a general idea from the following section describing the main groups of clothing available, and then to see for yourself how the various manufacturers have gone about resolving the design problems.

As well as being comfortable and protected, you also need to be conspicuous. The importance of this is quite clear: a vehicle driver failing to see a motorcyclist is a major factor in about one-third of all accidents involving motorcycles, and the proportion is highest around town in daylight. The bright, modern clothes now available certainly help you to be seen, and many incorporate reflective material as part of their styling. If you already own dark clothing you can add one of the red or yellow 'dayglo' waistcoats available from accessory shops, or a fluorescent belt of Sam Brown pattern with a diagonal strap over the shoulder.

Choosing your clothing

Despite the range of new plastic and nylon materials now used for motorcycle clothing, the oldest answer to the problem of keeping out wind and rain is still quite the most effective – the two-piece waxed cotton oversuit. Introduced originally by Barbour but now widely imitated, these garments are still the only choice for many motorcyclists. A four-pocket jacket reaching to the hips and elastic-waisted trousers are very effective in keeping

out all water, and retain warmth reasonably well. However, the material does need reproofing from time to time. It amuses users of the waxed cotton suit, who were accustomed to being barred from pubs because their protective clothing made the chairs greasy, that nowadays the Barbour jacket has become the uniform of green-wellied yuppies.

This type of two-piece suit, sometimes called a trials suit, is also made in nylon: while this material is cheaper and more stylish for some tastes, it is not as effective as waxed cotton. Trials suits outsell all the other options because they are reasonably convenient and very effective at keeping out the cold and damp. It is worth considering those with a detachable lining which can be removed for summer use.

Although similar to a trials suit, the continental suit usually has a shorter jacket with elastic in the waist, and higher-waisted trousers held up by braces. While there are many variations in style, fastenings and pockets, all provide good draught-proofing from the tight waist. A bonus for some riders is that the jackets look smart when worn on their own. The more lightweight continental suits are often bought to be worn both on and off the bike, although they might not provide enough warmth on a long journey in cold weather. Before choosing from all the styles, colours, weights and lining thicknesses of continental or trials suits, consider your needs – the proportion of long and short journeys you will cover in winter and summer – and buy a suit which will fit over or under the other clothes you intend to wear.

These same considerations apply to one-piece suits, which are available in waxed cotton, nylon or other

A headlamp will help other road users to see you coming, and a tail light helps indicate your presence to motorists coming up from behind, while a fluorescent 'Sam Brown' belt like the one worn in the picture (below) will also help, day and night.

plastics. There are heavy-duty and lined versions, together with lightweight types most frequently chosen as a waterproof layer over other clothes. One-piece suits tend to look bulky when you are walking around as they have to be made with enough material in the seat to allow knees to be bent and back to be leaned forward when you are riding. They are usually as warm as more expensive two-piece equivalents, but they take more time to put on and take off. Most riders who use one-piece suits acknowledge that they cannot always keep out all water on a long journey in hard rain, but they can still prove very effective when worn with suitable clothes underneath.

The most expensive options available to you are one-piece or two-piece leather suits, which are durable, comfortable and stylish. For the riders who choose them, however, their greatest advantage is their resistance to abrasion, which appeals to anyone conscious of the fact that he may one day find himself sliding along a hard road – or, for a racing motorcyclist, a hard racetrack. You can buy a leather suit off the peg or made to measure: in either case, look for a snug fit to prevent billowing in a one-piece and draughts in a two-piece, and make sure that the sleeves are long enough. Remember that leather is not the best material for keeping out the cold and will not remain waterproof for more than an hour or so in rain. A thin one-piece oversuit may also be needed for wet weather, while winter conditions may require something heavier as well.

New-generation suits incorporating 'Gore-tex' are as expensive as most leather suits but considerably more versatile. For the first time, motorcyclists (as well as climbers and others who require outdoor protection) have a material available which guarantees 100 per cent impermeability, yet can breathe so that condensation and sweating are prevented. Pioneered by BMW, who incorporated protective padding at strategic points, suits offering 'Gore-tex' protection are now available from several manufacturers, such as Yoko, Rukka, Jumbo International and Alpine. Use of this wonder fabric now extends to gloves and mittens, and even a liner for leather boots. If money is no object, it is possible to remain dry and comfortable from fingertips to toes.

Summing up the suit situation, a waxed cotton two-piece is probably the best answer for serious winter riding. For local commuting, where you perhaps have a train or bus alternative in the worst weather, an anorak and plastic over-trousers should be sufficient. Between these extremes, choose the compromise which best meets your needs and pocket: you will probably end up with combinations of suits which can be used with tee-shirts and pullovers to deal with a variety of riding conditions. Whatever you choose, check that the details – zips, velcro strips, pockets, waterpoof flaps, seam linings, colour, style – suit your taste and seem capable of withstanding hard use.

You also need clothing to cover the bits of you which a suit does not protect. To keep your neck warm and dry where helmet and collar meet, wear a woollen or silk scarf, or a balaclava (particularly useful when using an open-face helmet) made of wool or cotton. Always wear gloves, to protect your hands in an accident as well as to keep them warm. Thin, unlined leather gloves provide the most comfort and best control in hot weather; lined leather gloves or mittens (mittens are generally warmer than gloves) should cope with colder conditions; and in wet weather waxed cotton or plastic over-mittens worn on top of lined or unlined gloves are best. When dressing yourself up for winter riding, take care not to end up with so many layers of material over your hands that you have difficulty in feeling and operating the controls – remember, however, that frozen fingers are not very sensitive either.

Considerations of safety and comfort also affect your choice for foot protection. Strong shoes or boots are essential. As well as leaving your feet vulnerable in an accident, ordinary shoes or trainers will make them cold and wet in rain, and the upper part of the left shoe will soon disintegrate against the gear-shift. Durable leather boots and thick woollen socks are the answer for many riders, but remember that leather starts to let in water after an hour's riding, even if the zips do not leak before this. For a long journey in rain, waxed cotton, plastic or rubber over-shoes are reasonably effective at keeping feet dry. Thin wellingtons are another idea for summer rain, but they are cold in winter.

Dispatch riders, and others who cover long distances in all weathers, resort to another aid to riding comfort: electrically heated gloves, socks and waistcoats. For one IAM member who thinks nothing of riding from London to Edinburgh and back on a 24-hour business trip, electrically heated clothing makes bearable hundreds of miles in wintery conditions which otherwise could not be tolerated. For less dedicated motorcyclists, electrically heated grips are a luxury worth indulging in if cold weather riding is their choice.

Summary

- Effective clothing serves four important functions: it keeps you *warm, dry, protected in an accident* and *conspicuous*.
- Study the *huge variety of outfits* on the market before deciding which suits your needs and pocket; remember that feet and hands need good protection too.

24

HELMETS

As it is compulsory for all motorcycle and moped riders to wear a proper safety helmet, how should you go about choosing this important piece of equipment from the bewildering range of styles, types, materials, prices and standards to be found in accessory shops? You may ask the advice of a motorcycling friend, but remember that there is no guarantee that a design which suits him will be comfortable for you. As with the clothing described in the previous chapter, our advice can only be that you read on to find out the general options available to you, then spend time at a shop narrowing down your choice, on the grounds of comfort and price, from the 70 or so varieties on the market.

Helmet styles

Since shapes vary and sizes are inconsistent between one manufacturer and another, take plenty of time and keep trying on different helmets of your chosen type and price range until you find the one which fits best. A good, comfortable fit really is the most important consideration: a helmet costing £200 and made to the highest standards will not protect you properly in an accident unless it fits well. The snuggest fit which will cause no discomfort, even during a long journey, is what you should aim for. All helmets on the British market will offer the necessary level of protection because they have to survive repeated and stringent testing in the laboratories of the British

Standards Institute. These procedures ensure that the helmet you buy will withstand repeated blows, resist penetration by sharp objects and have a strong enough strap to cope with the most severe impacts.

Three different materials with varying characteristics – glass-fibre, polycarbonate plastic and ABS plastic – have been used in recent years for helmet shells. Glass-fibre is considered the best, although it is more expensive and slightly heavier; polycarbonate plastic is cheaper because it lends itself to mass production, but its limitations mean that its popularity is declining. Unlike a glass-fibre helmet, a polycarbonate plastic one must *never* be painted or covered with stickers because it can be weakened by some solvents and chemicals. The two types respond differently on impact. Glass-fibre flexes to absorb energy and then starts to break up so that it will show marks after a crash; polycarbonate plastic deforms elastically and reverts to its original shape so that no damage shows. A polycarbonate helmet, therefore, ought to be replaced after a very hard knock even if there is no visible sign of damage. ABS plastic is dropping out of general use because helmets of this material have to be very thick and heavy to meet the current British Standard.

Besides choosing your material, you are faced with the choice of a full-face or open-face style. The chief advantages of the full-face (or integral) style are that it offers better face and chin protection in an accident and excellent weather protection in normal riding. On the other hand, some riders find them claustrophobic to wear; they can also be lifted uncomfortably at high speed and tend to be more expensive. Only you can decide which type you prefer.

Some authorities recommend that a helmet should be replaced after four years' use, since the slight weakening which occurs with age and exposure to the elements can reduce its protective qualities. This may seem extravagant, especially if you find an old helmet comfortable, but ask yourself how much importance you attach to your head – probably a fair bit. Your helmet, needless to say, should also be looked after carefully so that it never drops on to the ground or comes into contact with chemicals or solvents which might weaken it.

Straps, visors and goggles

Since you must always fasten your helmet securely to make sure that it will stay on your head in an accident, it is worth paying attention to the design of buckles or fastenings on the strap. They need to be easy to use, as it becomes irritating to have to struggle with a strap every time you begin or complete a journey. Check the ease of adjustment if the helmet is to be used by more than one person – by a pillion passenger, for example – to remove the risk of someone wearing it insecurely. Chin straps are normally made of nylon, but leather (which has better resistance to fire) is also used for this purpose. If the wearer of a helmet has a chin cup fitted, it is now a legal requirement that this cup is worn on a secondary chin strap, which will have to be added if the helmet has only one strap. As well as being illegal, wearing a chin cup on a single-strap helmet has proved to be dangerous in the event of a tumble.

Good eye protection is vital, and the BS4110 standard is now accepted by all thinking riders as reasonable, whatever the problems surrounding its introduction. Riding with neither visor nor goggles is extremely foolish, since road grit, stones or glass can be thrown into your eyes by other traffic even when riding slowly over a short distance. Goggles and visors need to keep out draughts and be durable – scuffs and scratches can dangerously impair your vision, particularly at night. It is worth spending money on the best possible equipment, as good lenses, whether made of glass or polycarbonate, are more resistant to scratching. Look after visors and goggles carefully: sponging them with warm, soapy water will keep them scrupulously clean. Avoid wiping them with gloved fingers while on the road in wet weather because you will scratch the surface as you move the film of dirty water around. Water should be blown off a clear, clean surface but, if you do have difficulty with vision, stop and clean the visor or goggles properly.

The detachable peaks and visors made for open-face helmets are quite effective as sun-shields and air deflectors in town, but they tend to be lifted badly by wind pressure at higher speeds.

Summary

- Choose a *full-face* or *open-face* helmet which fits you comfortably and snugly: a good fit is the most important consideration.
- Look after your *visor* or *goggles* carefully: good visibility depends on keeping lenses clean and clear. Make sure that your eye protection complies with BS4110 in all respects.

25

TOURING ABROAD

For many motorcyclists, the greatest pleasure of their chosen means of transport comes with a touring holiday abroad. By keeping off busy trunk roads, autoroutes, autostradas and autobahns, you can follow quiet highways which carry much less traffic than you usually find on our crowded island, and you can enjoy the delights of motorcycling in warm weather as you venture to the south of France, Italy or Spain. There is no reason why a competent motorcyclist should not feel perfectly confident when riding in an unfamiliar country, on the 'wrong' side of the road. Even busy cities such as Paris and Rome – with their reputation for devil-may-care traffic – should hold no fears as long as the basic rules of advanced motorcycling are followed.

Planning ahead

Just like any other aspect of advanced motorcycling, you should plan ahead to make the most of a journey to the southern sun. When you have decided on your destination, buy the appropriate large-scale road maps from any good bookshop. The Michelin series, which cover the whole of Europe, are among the best, and these are also now available as high-quality atlases of France or Europe, published by Hamlyn. If you are in a hurry to get to the beach you may choose to use motorways, but remember that tolls are charged in France, Switzerland and Italy. If you have time, it is much more enjoyable to plan a leisurely journey on quieter roads.

A good way of planning a route is to draw a pencil line on the map between your ferry arrival port and your destination, and then ink in a route along roads – choosing plenty of secondary roads if your journey time allows it – running close to the pencil line. Choosing smaller roads will force you to allow more time for the trip, but it will provide a delightful and relaxing way to see the country, and its towns and villages. A pillion passenger will appreciate riding through more interesting surroundings.

Unless you are travelling unusually light, panniers are invaluable for packing all your belongings, keeping them dry and ensuring even weight distribution. A tank bag is useful for storing items such as maps and guidebooks which are needed during a day's run, although it can obscure the instruments on some types of bike. Shoving all your worldly goods in plastic bags and tying them to the saddle or a carrier with 'bungee' straps just will not work: even if you do not lose the lot in the first town, the weight and wind action at the rear will make the bike unstable. Theft is a problem wherever you go, particularly further to the south, so use lockable panniers and try not to leave luggage unattended. When you see the way that many European motorcyclists tether their machines to lamp-posts with a chain stout enough to anchor a ship, you will realise the wisdom of taking a secure padlock and chain to augment your bike's fork lock.

As you will probably be covering a considerable mileage in a relatively short time, you must be adequately clothed – getting soaked to the skin in the first hour will ruin the whole of a long day's riding. Even if you are heading for the Mediterranean in summer, you may encounter plenty of cold winds and rain through the northern miles before temperatures start to rise, and you can be caught out by severe thunderstorms anywhere. Start out with waterproof and warm clothing, which is easy to take off on a sunny day but hard to do without on a cold and wet one.

As far as insurance is concerned, you should tell your insurer or broker where you are going and arrange a Green Card. Your normal insurance arrangements – fully comprehensive if you have any sense – should be extended to cover you while you are abroad. Extra cover is not legally required when travelling in EC countries, but the basic cover provided automatically is a bare minimum. You will have enough to worry about, in the unfortunate event of an accident or breakdown abroad, without having the extra headache of the cost. As well as making travel arrangements through their organisations, AA and RAC members can take advantage of particularly good insurance packages which cover your bike's return to Britain if you are unlucky enough to suffer a major breakdown or an accident. It would also be worth taking out insurance to cover health care and theft, no matter how remote these possibilities may seem, and the E111 from obtained from your local DHSS office will give you basic health cover in the EC.

Differences to watch for

The moment when you ride off the ferry and into another country is always exciting. At first you will keep reminding yourself to ride on the right, and multi-lingual warning signs along the road leaving the ferry terminal will reinforce your awareness. This should ensure that you get used to travelling on the 'wrong' side of the road without mishap for the first few miles, but the trouble can come later when you have gained some experience and feel more confident. It is all too easy, when there is no traffic to remind you, to forget momentarily that you must ride on the right. The time to be on your guard is whenever you stop, particularly if you do so on the left-hand side of the road. It may seem quite natural to come out of a shop or filling station, get on your machine and set off up the road on the *left*.

Apart from the self-evident fact that you ride on the other side, most continental traffic rules are the same as British ones, with one important exception which we shall examine in a moment. Traffic signs present no worries – Britain adopted the international pattern long ago, and the few local pecularities can generally be deciphered by using common sense and a little imagination. One sign to watch for in France is 'chaussée deformée' (deformed road), which definitely means what it says: beware of savage bumps in a surface which still seems to be settling after a recent earthquake! You might also see in France a red warning triangle sign bearing the silhouette of a frog: yes, it means that you must beware of frogs on the road, because the surface will be treacherous if large numbers of these slippery creatures have been squashed by traffic.

You need to be watchful of road surface quality, as th
standard in most European countries is not a match fo
British roads. Surfaces can be terrible on smaller roads
particularly in France and Spain, and cambers can be
more awkward and kerbs less clearly marked. Coping
with the cobbles and avoiding the tramlines found in some
towns and cities can need all your concentration when you
are dealing also with fast-moving traffic on the 'wrong' side
of the road *and* trying to find your way.

You need to be extra careful in spotting traffic light
because they are often suspended from overhead cables
with a small 'reminder' set at eye level to the right for the
person first in a queue. In some countries the ambe
intermediate stage is omitted, and you tend to find fa
more filter systems (for left, right and straight on). A
continuously flashing amber light is frequently used, bu
need cause no confusion: it simply means that you should
cross a particularly hazardous junction with great caution
and be prepared to give way.

The important exception to British traffic rule
mentioned earlier is the notorious 'priority to the right
rule, seen at its most virulent in France. Thankfully, the
French authorities, motivated by having one of the highes
road accident rates in Europe, are at last trying to sort ou
the dangers of their 'priority to the right' policy, but you
must still be on your guard. Roundabouts can cause
confusion because the traditional French system is th
opposite to ours, meaning that traffic on the roundabou
must give way to traffic coming in from the right at each
entrance road. All this is in the process of changing, with
many roundabouts now having white lines to indicate tha
incoming traffic must give way in the normal manner, bu
always be prepared to find the old system operating.

The same wisdom applies to traffic in towns or on
country roads. It has always been necessary in France to
expect a *Deux Chevaux* to come hurtling into your path
from any side road to the right. Although better use o
white line give-way markings is now being made to
establish a more logical system of priority, you will still find
local drivers joining a major road from the right withou
even slowing down or looking to see if it is clear, trusting to
luck that any oncoming traffic will give way. You need to

e especially cautious in towns, because 'priority to the ight' applies at any junction without traffic lights or ive-way road markings. Only when travelling along a najor road dotted with yellow diamond 'you have priority' igns can you be reasonably sure that a vehicle will not merge from a side road to the right.

In addition to this warning, there are a few other spects of continental motorcycling which require special are. These are mentioned to help you enjoy your uropean touring holiday, and not with the aim of putting ou off.

Continental policemen, especially the motorcycle olice in France, tend to take a much harder line than heir British counterparts with erring motorcyclists. They vill listen to no excuses about ignorance of the law in their ountry, and invariably they will deal with a nisdeameanour committed by a British rider in the implest way – by demanding an on-the-spot fine. Their ystem is well organised, with all major credit cards ccepted! Make sure you understand the speed limits in ach country you enter, because a speeding offence is the nost common reason for being stopped. There is one mportant point about German autobahns: although they re the only motorways in Europe without an overall peed limit, 100kph (60mph) 120kph (75mph) limits *are* ften posted for short stretches, sometimes for no obvious eason. They can appear by surprise, but take note of how igidly the locals obey them – the fines for not doing so are eavy.

The yellow headlight, fitted to French motorcycles as vell as all other vehicles, is intended to prevent dazzle which is achieved simply by cutting down the amount of ight passing through the headlight glass, not through any pecial properties of the colour yellow). A visitor does not eed to modify his ordinary white headlight, but it is dvisable to apply black marking sections to the headlight ens to minimise annoyance to the locals. It is *compulsory* or motorcyclists to ride with the headlight on day and ight in most European countries.

Your motorcycle needs to be in good fettle before you eave for the continent: either carry out a full service ourself or take your machine to a dealer and tell him why

a thorough job must be done. Any suspect cables should b
replaced, tyres should be in good condition (punctures ar
a nuisance at the best of times, but worse on an empty roa
with a bike loaded high with luggage) and any tire
components, such as a worn clutch, should be replace
before you leave home. All you really need for the journe
is a normal tool kit, chain lubricant and a set of spar
bulbs. If you do take irons and a puncture repair outfi
remember to include a pump or trials-type inflator an
your usual pocket pressure gauge. It is a good idea t
obtain a list of continental dealers which handle your mak
of machine, and a phrase book listing common mechanic
terms might help if you would be struggling with languag
in the event of a breakdown.

Of course, you may be considering a journey furthe
afield. It is quite common for riders these days to tackl
awe-inspiring expeditions, like crossing Africa or ridin
around India. This is advanced riding all right, but beyon
the scope of this book.

Summary

- *Plan ahead* as far as possible so that before you leav
  home you have a good idea of your route.
- Once your initial wariness about *riding on the rigl*
  has disappeared, it is easy to forget momentarily tha
  you are abroad; be especially careful not to ride awa
  on the left after a short stop at a filling station or shop
- Always be alert to the dangers of the '*priority to th
  right*' rule when riding in France.
- Use common sense and imagination to decipher an
  unfamiliar road signs; make sure you know the *spee
  limits* for the countries you visit.
- Do not think that *ignorance of the law* will ever b
  accepted as an excuse by continental traffic police.

26

NOW FOR THE TEST

Now that you have absorbed all the advice in this manual, and if you are not already a member of the Institute of Advanced Motorists, you must be wondering whether you have developed the ability to pass the advanced motorcycling test.

Just how good a rider are you? Very expert, you may think, but are you sure? You must remember that the Government L-test is only a very basic, elementary examination; the real learning starts when you can throw away your L-plates. Passing the ordinary motorcycling test is only a starting point in the acquisition of mature riding skills. Fortunately, many riders realise this, and there comes a time when they want to reassure themselves that their skills are developing along the right lines.

This is why the Institute of Advanced Motorists exists. It was founded in 1956 as a non-profit making organisation and is registered as a charity. It is dedicated to the promotion of road safety by encouraging motorists and motorcyclists to take pride in good driving and riding. By taking the IAM's test, riders can measure the progress they have made since passing the basic test.

The advanced motorcycling test

The test lasts for about 90 minutes and is something which any rider of reasonable experience and skill should be able to pass without difficulty. Whether candidates pass or fail, however, they learn a great deal from the examiners, who are all past or present police motorcyclists, Class One certificate holders with traffic patrol riding backgrounds.

Skill with responsibility is what the IAM aims to

promote. The number of road accidents – there are ove
300,000 casualties and over 5000 deaths every year – woul
drop dramatically if every driver and motorcyclist had th
ability to pass the IAM test and the self-discipline to adher
to its standards at all times. You have to pass the test t
become a member of the IAM.

The IAM was founded by motorists from all walks c
life with the common aim of making our roads safer b
raising driving standards. It is controlled by a Counc
whose members are elected as a result of their expertise i
various spheres of motoring and motorcycling. The
represent accident prevention authorities, medicine, th
industry and trade, the police, driving school:
magistrates, the motoring press, other motorin
organisations and the IAM's own area Groups.

Ever since it started, the IAM's activities have bee
endorsed by successive Transport Ministers. As an exper
organisation, its opinions on road safety issues ar
regularly sought by the Government. Indeed, one of it
main aims is to represent the views of skilled, responsibl
road users to the authorities. Each new membe:
therefore, becomes a valuable addition to the campaign fo
better standards on our roads.

The advanced motorcycling test was introduced i
1976 and has proved very popular indeed among riders.]
has been acclaimed by the motorcycle press, b
experienced riders of all ages, by road safety officials an
by the motorcycle clubs. More than 300,000 driving an
motorcyling tests have so far been carried out; 79 per cer
of the 7000 motorcyclists who have taken the test hav
passed and become members of the IAM. The Army ha
adopted the test at home and abroad, and more than 35
companies use the driving test as a stringent check on th
skills of staff using company-owned vehicles.

In 1980 the first full IAM Group was formed to cater fo
the needs of motorcyclists who are interested in advance
riding techniques. There are now nearly 50 motorcycl
groups and sections across Britain, and many of them ru
observer schemes to advise aspiring test candidates. Th
approaches vary from informal classroom sessions to or
the-road advice from skilled and experienced IAM
members who belong to observer teams. Very often thes

teams have the benefit of tuition from Class One police riders who are themselves group members, so one can expect a high degree of expertise. If you like the idea of joining a club whose main interest is in advanced riding, contact with your local group should be your first move. There are also some riding schools which offer intensive training on a one-to-one basis, but their courses tend to be relatively expensive compared with group participation.

What does the test involve?

A typical test route covers around 30 miles and incorporates all kinds of road conditions, including congested urban areas, main roads, narrow country lanes and residential streets. You are not expected to give a display of fancy riding – on the contrary, you should handle your machine in the steady, workmanlike way in which you ride every day. The examiners do not, for example, expect exaggeratedly slow speeds or excessive signalling. What they *do* want is to see candidates ride with due regard for road, traffic and weather conditions, and all speed limits must be observed. They will want to see you riding briskly and to ensure that you are not afraid to cruise at the legal limit when circumstances permit – progress with safety.

You will be asked to carry out certain manoeuvres at low speeds on a course through markers on an off-road site. There are no trick questions in the test and no attempts to catch you out. Throughout the test the examiner will be following you on his own machine, stopping at intervals to give you route instructions for the next part of the course. This is the 'pursuit' method used by the police for their own test. It has been found to be by far the most efficient way of maintaining a prolonged check on a rider's behaviour on the road.

Who can take the test?

Anyone with a full British licence, provided that he has not been convicted of a serious traffic offence in the last three years. You can take the test on almost any motorcycle which you provide yourself, as long as its capacity is over 200cc.

Where can I take the test?

Almost certainly quite near your home. The IAM has a nationwide network of test routes, as you will see from the list on page 176. The examiner will arrange a mutually acceptable date and time and meet you at a prearranged rendezvous.

Who are the examiners?

They are all holders of the Class One Police certificate. This means that they have passed the stiffest test of riding ability in Britain – the Police examination for traffic patrol motorcyclists.

Here in greater detail are some of the points the examiners look for and comment on in their test reports:

Acceleration
Smooth and progressive? Excessive or insufficient? Is acceleration used at the right time and place?

Braking
Smooth and progressive, or late and fierce? Are the brakes used in conjunction with mirror and/or signals? Are road, traffic and weather conditions taken into account?

Clutch control
Are engine and road speeds properly co-ordinated when changing gear? Does the candidate slip or ride the clutch? Does he coast with the clutch disengaged?

Gearchanging
Is it a smooth change action, without jerking?

Use of gears
Are the gears correctly selected and used? Is the right gear selected before reaching a hazard?

Riding position
Does the candidate sit astride his machine correctly, with his weight properly distributed and in a position from which he can properly control the motorcycle? Is the candidate alert?

Clothing
Is the candidate properly attired in helmet and with clothes suitable for motorcycling?

Observation
Does he 'read' the road ahead and show a good sense of anticipation? Does he show the ability to judge speed and distance?

Concentration
Does the rider keep his attention on the road? Does he allow himself to be distracted easily?

Maintaining progress
Bearing in mind the road, traffic and weather conditions, does the rider keep up a reasonable pace and maintain good progress?

Obstruction
Is the candidate careful not to obstruct other vehicles by riding too slowly, taking up the wrong position on the road, or failing to anticipate and react correctly to the traffic situation ahead?

Positioning
Does the rider keep to the correct part of the road, especially when approaching or negotiating hazards?

Lane discipline
Does he keep to the appropriate lane? Is he careful not to straddle white lines?

Observation of road surfaces
Does the rider keep an eye on the road surface, especially in bad weather, and does he watch out for slippery conditions?

Traffic signals
Are signals, signs and road markings observed, obeyed and approached correctly? Does the rider show courtesy at pedestrian crossings?

Speed limits and other legal requirements
Are they observed? (The examiner cannot condone breaches of the law.)

Overtaking
Is this carried out safely and decisively, maintaining the right distance from other vehicles and using the mirror, signals and gears correctly?

Hazard procedure and cornering
Are road and traffic hazards coped with properly? Are bends and corners taken in the right manner?

Mirror
Does the candidate frequently use the mirror? Does he use it in conjunction with his signals and before changing speed or course? Does he use rear observation when required?

Signals
Are turn indicator signals – and hand ones when needed – given at the right place and in good time? Are the horn and headlight used in accordance with the *Highway Code*?

Restraint
Does the candidate show reasonable restraint – but not indecision?

Consideration
Is sufficient consideration and courtesy shown to other road users?

Machine sympathy
Does he treat the motorcycle with care? Does he overstress it, perhaps by revving the engine needlessly or by fierce braking?

Manoeuvring
Finally, are manoeuvres performed smoothly and competently?

Results

At the end of the test your examiner will, after announcing your result, give an expert view of your skill and responsibility as a motorcyclist. There may be praise, and certainly constructive criticism will be offered – the IAM aims to be entirely honest with you. Occasionally, a candidate is found to have developed a potentially dangerous fault of which he is completely unaware; a quiet word from the examiner will help him to correct it. You will not be failed for minor faults.

When you pass

When you pass the advanced test and become a member of the IAM, these are among the benefits available to you:

- *Badge*: The right to display the IAM's badge and certificate, providing visible proof of the standard you have set yourself.
- *Insurance*: An introduction to insurers who may give special terms, subject to a satisfactory proposal.
- *Magazine*: A magazine, *Milestones*, which is published every four months. It is produced especially for IAM members and written by and for people who take a keen interest in motoring and motorcycling.
- *Social activities*: The chance to meet other men and women who share your outlook on motorcycling. You can decide to join one of the IAM's local groups and take part in the events which they organise.

The Institute of Advanced Motorists is based at IAM House, 359 Chiswick High Road, London W4 4HS; telephone: 01-994 4403 (24-hour answering service).

LIST OF TEST ROUTES

This is a list of the test routes operated by the IAM at the time of going to press. You can take the advanced test anywhere you like in the UK, and almost certainly quite close to your home. For further information, contact the IAM.

Aberdeen	Cardiff	Greenock
Aylesbury	Carlisle	Grimsby
Ayr	Chelmsford	Guildford
Banff	Cheltenham	Harrogate
Bangor	Chester	Hartlepool
Barnsley	Chichester	Haverfordwest
Bedford	Chorley	Hereford
Belfast	Colwyn Bay	Huddersfield
Berwick-on-Tweed	Coventry	Hull
Birkenhead	Crawley	Huntly
Birmingham	Crewe	Inverness
Blackpool	Darlington	Ipswich
Bodmin	Debenham	Isle of Man
Bolton	Derby	Isle of Wight
Boston	Dorchester	Kendal
Bournemouth	Dumfries	Kettering
Bradford	Dundee	Ladybank
Bridgend	Dunoon	Leeds
Brighton	Edinburgh	Leicester
Bristol	Elgin	Lichfield
Bude	Exeter	Lincoln
Burton-on-Trent	Folkestone	Liverpool
Bury St Edmunds	Galashiels	Londonderry
Cambridge	Glasgow	Luton
Canterbury	Grantham	Maidstone

Manchester
Mansfield
Middlesborough
Newark
Newcastle
Newmarket
Newport
Northampton
Norwich
Nottingham
Oban
Okehampton
Oxford
Penrith
Perth
Peterborough
Plymouth
Porthmadog
Portsmouth
Preston
Reading
Retford
Ripon
Rotherham
Scarborough
Scunthorpe
Sheffield

Shrewsbury
Southampton
Southend
St Austell
St Helens
Staines
Stockport
Stoke-on-Trent
Stowmarket
Sunderland
Swansea
Swindon
Taunton
Truro
Tunbridge Wells
Wakefield
Walsall
Watford
Wetherby
Wick
Widnes
Wigan
Winchester
Windsor
Woking
Wolverhampton
Worcester

Worksop
Worthing
Yeovil
York

London
Barnes
Crystal Palace
Harrow
Wanstead

West Germany
(HM Forces and British nationals only)
Bielefeld
Gutersloh
Hanover
Paderborn
Rheindahlen
Sennelager

Cyprus
(HM Forces and British nationals only)
Akrotiri
Larnaca

SIGNS AND
SIGNALS

Traffic signs SIGNS GIVING ORDERS

These signs are mostly circular and those with red circles are mostly prohibitive

Maximum speed

National speed limit applies

Stop and Give Way

Give way to traffic on major road

School crossing patrol

No vehicles

No entry for vehicular traffic

No right turn

No left turn

No U turns

No overtaking

Give priority to vehicles from opposite direction

No motor vehicles

No motor vehicles except solo motorcycles, scooters or mopeds

Manually operated temporary 'STOP' sign

No vehicles with over 12 seats except regular scheduled, school and works buses

No cycling

No pedestrians

No goods vehicles over maximum gross weight shown (in tonnes)

No vehicles including load over weight shown (in tonnes)

Axle weight limit in tonnes

No vehicles over height shown

No vehicle or combination of vehicles over length shown

No vehicles over width shown

No stopping (Clearway)

Permit holders only
Parking restricted to use by people named on sign

URBAN CLEARWAY Monday to Friday
am 8·9·30   pm 4·30 6·30
No stopping during times shown except for as long as necessary to set down or pick up passengers

Plates below some signs qualify their message

End
End of restriction

Except for loading
Exception for loading/unloading goods

Except buses and coaches
Exception for vehicles with over 12 seats

Except buses
Exception for stage and scheduled express carriages, school and works buses

Except for access
Exception for access to premises and land adjacent to the road where there is no alternative route

Signs with blue circles but no red border mostly give positive instruction

Ahead only

Turn left ahead (right if symbol reversed)

Turn left (right if symbol reversed)

Keep left (right if symbol reversed)

Vehicles may pass either side to reach same destination

Route to be used by pedal cycles only

Minimum speed

End of minimum speed

Mini-roundabout (roundabout circulation – give way to vehicles from the immediate right)

One-way traffic (Note: compare circular "Ahead only" sign)

Shared pedal cycle and pedestrian route

With-flow bus and cycle lane

Contra-flow bus lane

With-flow pedal cycle lane

WARNING SIGNS *Mostly triangular*

STOP
100 yds

Distance to
"STOP"
line ahead

Cross roads

Roundabout

T junction

Staggered junction

GIVE WAY
50 yds

Distance to
"Give Way"
line ahead

Double bend
first to left
(may be reversed)

REDUCE
SPEED
NOW

Plate below
some signs

Sharp deviation
of route to left
(or right if
chevrons reversed)

Bend to right
(or left if symbol reversed)

Dual carriageway
ends

Slippery road

Two-way traffic
straight ahead

Two-way traffic
crosses
one-way road

Traffic merges from left/right
with equal priority

Road narrows on
right (left if
symbol reversed)

Road narrows
on both sides

Elderly
people

Crossing point
for elderly
people (blind or
disabled if shown)

No footway
for 400 yds

Pedestrians in
road ahead

Pedestrian
crossing

School

Children going to
or from school

Patrol

School crossing
patrol ahead
(Some signs have
amber lights which
flash when
patrol is operating)

Uneven road

Traffic
signals

Failure of
light signals

Steep hill
downwards

Steep hill
upwards

Gradients may be shown as a ratio
i.e. 20% = 1:5

Risk of Grounding

Risk of grounding
of long low
vehicles at
level crossing

Road works

Hump bridge

Change to opposite
carriageway
(may be reversed)

Loose
chippings

Ford

Worded warning
sign

AUTOMATIC
BARRIERS
STOP
when
lights show

Plate to indicate
a level crossing
equipped with
automatic barriers
and flashing lights

Level crossing
with barrier
or gate ahead

Level crossing
without barrier
or gate ahead

Level crossing
without barrier
(the additional
lower half of the cross
is used when there
is more than one
railway line)

Cycle route ahead

Height limit
(e.g. low bridge)

Available width of headroom
indicated

Opening or swing
bridge ahead

Quayside or
river bank

Overhead electric
cable; plate
indicates maximum
height of vehicles
which can pass
safely

Cattle

Wild animals

Wild horses
or ponies

Accompanied
horses or ponies
crossing the
road ahead

Other danger;
plate indicates
nature of
danger

Distance to
tunnel

Falling or
fallen rocks

Low-flying
aircraft or sudden
aircraft noise

Distance over
which road
humps extend

DIRECTION SIGNS
Signs on motorways
Mostly rectangular
Blue backgrounds

Start of motorway and point
from which motorway
regulations apply

On approaches to junctions
(junction number on black background)

Route confirmatory sign
after junction

End of motorway

At a junction leading directly into a motorway

Downward pointing arrows mean
"Get in lane"

The panel with the sloping arrow
indicates the destinations which can be
reached by leaving the motorway
at the next junction

On approaches to junctions

On approaches to junctions (The blue panel indicates that the motorway commences from the junction ahead. The motorway shown in brackets can also be reached by proceeding in that direction)

Signs on primary routes
Green backgrounds

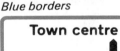

At the junction

Route confirmatory sign after junction

Route confirmatory sign after junction

Signs on non-primary routes
Black borders

On approaches to junctions (a symbol may sometimes be shown to indicate a warning of a hazard or prohibition on a road leading from a junction)

At the junction

On approaches to junctions

At the junction

Direction to camping and caravan site

Holiday route

Diversion route

Direction to toilets with access for the disabled

Picnic site

Advisory route for lorries

Recommended route for pedal cycles to place shown

Local direction signs
Blue borders

On approaches to junctions (where there is a different route for pedal cycles this may be shown in a blue panel)

Tourist attraction

Ancient monument in the care of English Heritage

Route for pedestrians

Airport

INFORMATION SIGNS *All rectangular*

Entrance to
controlled
parking zone

One-way street

Priority over vehicles
from opposite
direction

Advance warning of
restriction or prohibition
ahead

No through
road

Hospital
ahead

Distance to service area with fuel,
parking and cafeteria facilities
(The current petrol price may be shown
in pence per gallon or litre,
or may be omitted)

End of
controlled
parking zone

Appropriate traffic lanes
at junction ahead

"Count-down" markers at exit from motorway
(each bar represents 100 yards to the exit).
Green-backed markers may be used on primary
routes and white-backed markers with red bars
on the approaches to concealed level crossings

Recommended route
for pedal cycles

Tourist
information
point

Permanent
reduction in
available lanes,
e.g. two-lane
carriageway
reducing to one

Temporary lane closure

The number and position of arrows and red
bars may be varied according to lanes open
and closed

Bus lane on road
at junction ahead

Lane control signals

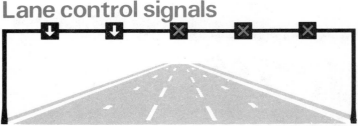

White arrow — lane available to traffic facing the sign. Red crosses — lane closed to traffic facing the sign.

Light signals controlling traffic

TRAFFIC LIGHT SIGNALS

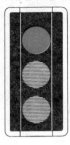 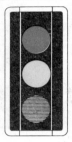  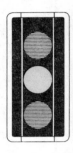

RED means "Stop". Wait behind the stop line on the carriageway.

RED AND AMBER also means "Stop". Do not pass through or start until GREEN shows.

GREEN means you may go on if the way is clear. Take special care if you mean to turn left or right and give way to pedestrians who are crossing.

AMBER means "Stop" at the stop line. You may go on only if the AMBER appears after you have crossed the stop line or are so close to it that to pull up might cause an accident.

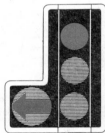

A GREEN ARROW may be provided in addition to the full green signal if movement in a certain direction is allowed before or after the full green phase. If the way is clear you may go but only in the direction shown by the arrow. You may do this whatever other lights may be showing.

FLASHING RED LIGHTS

Alternately flashing red lights mean YOU MUST STOP

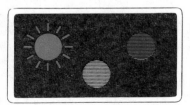

At level crossings, lifting bridges, airfields, fire stations, etc

Road markings

ACROSS THE CARRIAGEWAY

Give way to traffic on major road

Give way to traffic from the right in roundabout

Give way to traffic from right at mini-roundabout

Stop line at "STOP" sign

Stop line at signals or police control

ALONG THE CARRIAGEWAY

Double white lines   **Diagonal stripes**   **Lane markings**

See Rules 71 and 72   See Rule 73   Lane line   Centre line   Hazard
                                              See Rules   warning line
                                              74 and 75   See Rule 70

ALONG THE EDGE OF THE CARRIAGEWAY
Waiting restrictions

No waiting on carriageway, pavement or verge (except to load or unload or while passengers board or alight) at times shown on nearby plates or on entry signs to controlled parking zones.

If no days are indicated on the sign, the restrictions are in force every day including Sundays and Bank Holidays. The lines give a guide to the restriction in force but the time plates must be consulted.

Examples of plates
indicating restriction times

No waiting
for at least
eight hours
between 7 am and
7 pm on four or more
days of the week

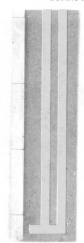

No waiting for at
least eight hours
between 7 am and
7 pm on four or more
days of the week
plus some additional
period outside
these times

During any
other periods

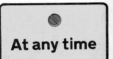

Continuous prohibition

Plate giving times

Limited waiting

ON THE KERB OR AT THE EDGE OF THE CARRIAGEWAY
Loading restrictions

No loading or unloading at times shown on nearby plates. If no days are indicated on the sign the restrictions are in force every day including Sundays and Bank Holidays.

During every working day

For example

During every working day,
and additional times

For example

During any other periods

For example

No loading
Mon-Fri
8·00-9·30 am
4·30-6·30 pm

ZEBRA CONTROLLED AREAS

OTHER ROAD MARKINGS

Keep entrance clear of stationary vehicles, even if picking up or setting down children

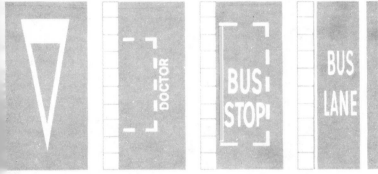

Warning of "Give Way"
just ahead

Parking space reserved
for vehicles named

See Rule 124

See Rule 82

Box junction
See Rule 99

Do not block entrance
to side road

Indication of traffic lanes

Note: Although *The Highway Code* shows many of the signs commonly in use, a comprehensive explanation of our signing system is given in the Department's booklet *Know Your Traffic Signs*, which is on sale at booksellers. The booklet also illustrates and explains the vast majority of signs the road user is likely to encounter.
The signs illustrated in *The Highway Code* are not all drawn to the same scale. In Wales, bilingual versions of some signs are used.